instant manager

taking control of work and life

institute

inspiring leaders

project
MANAGEMENT

PHIL BAGULEY

700034755466

PART OF HACHETTE LIVRE UK

The publisher has used its best endeavours to ensure that the URLs for external websites referred to in this book are correct and active at the time of going to press. However, the publisher and the author have no responsibility for the websites and can make no guarantee that a site will remain live or that the content will remain relevant, decent or appropriate.

Orders: Please contact Bookpoint Ltd, 130 Milton Park, Abingdon, Oxon OX14 4SB. Telephone: (44) 01235 827720, Fax: (44) 01235 400454. Lines are open from 9.00 to 5.00, Monday to Saturday, with a 24-hour message answering service. You can also order through our website www.hoddereducation.co.uk.

British Library Cataloguing in Publication Data
A catalogue record for this title is available from the British Library.

ISBN-13: 978 0340 968 765

First published	2008
Impression number	10 9 8 7 6 5 4 3 2 1
Year	2012 2011 2010 2009 2008

Typeset by Transet Limited, Coventry, England.
Printed in Great Britain for Hodder Education, an Hachette Livre UK Company, 338 Euston Road, London NW1 3BH, by CPI Cox & Wyman, Reading, Berkshire RG1 8EX.

Hachette Livre UK's policy is to use papers that are natural, renewable and recyclable products and made from wood grown in sustainable forests. The logging and manufacturing processes are expected to conform to the environmental regulations of the country of origin.

The Chartered Management Institute

chartered management institute

inspiring leaders

The Chartered Management Institute is the only chartered professional body that is dedicated to management and leadership. We are committed to raising the performance of business by championing management.

We represent 71,000 individual managers and have 450 corporate members. Within the Institute there are also a number of distinct specialisms, including the Institute of Business Consulting and Women in Management Network.

We exist to help managers tackle the management challenges they face on a daily basis by raising the standard of management in the UK. We are here to help individuals become better managers and companies develop better managers.

We do this through a wide range of products and services, from practical management checklists to tailored training and qualifications. We produce research on the latest 'hot' management issues, provide a vast array of useful information through our online management information centre, as well as offering consultancy services and career information.

You can access these resources 'off the shelf' or we can provide solutions just for you. Our range of products and services is designed to ensure companies and managers develop their potential and excel. Whether you are at the start of your career or a proven performer in the boardroom, we have something for you.

We engage policy makers and opinion formers and, as the leading authority on management, we are regularly consulted on a range of management issues. Through our in-depth research and regular policy surveys of members, we have a deep understanding of the latest management trends.

For more information visit our website **www.managers.org.uk** or call us on **01536 207307**.

Chartered Manager

Transform the way you work

The Chartered Management Institute's Chartered Manager award is the ultimate accolade for practising professional managers. Designed to transform the way you think about your work and how you add value to your organisation, it is based on demonstrating measurable impact.

This unique award proves your ability to make a real difference in the workplace.

Chartered Manager focuses on the six vital business skills of:

- Leading people
- Managing change
- Meeting customer needs
- Managing information and knowledge
- Managing activities and resources
- Managing yourself

Transform your organisation

There is a clear and well-established link between good management and improved organisational performance. Recognising this, the Chartered Manager scheme requires individuals to demonstrate how they are applying their leadership and change management skills to make significant impact within their organisation.

Transform your career

Whatever career stage a manager is at Chartered Manager will set them apart. Chartered Manager has proven to be a stimulus to career progression, either via recognition by their current employer or through the motivation to move on to more challenging roles with new employers.

But don't take just our word for it …

Chartered Manager has transformed the careers and organisations of managers in all sectors.

- *'Being a Chartered Manager was one of the main contributing factors which led to my recent promotion.'*
  Lloyd Ross, Programme Delivery Manager, British Nuclear Fuels

- *'I am quite sure that a part of the reason for my success in achieving my appointment was due to my Chartered Manager award which provided excellent, independent evidence that I was a high quality manager.'*
  Donaree Marshall, Head of Programme Management Office, Water Service, Belfast

- *'The whole process has been very positive, giving me confidence in my strengths as a manager but also helping me to identify the areas of my skills that I want to develop. I am delighted and proud to have the accolade of Chartered Manager.'*
  Allen Hudson, School Support Services Manager, Dudley Metropolitan County Council

- *'As we are in a time of profound change, I believe that I have, as a result of my change management skills, been able to provide leadership to my staff. Indeed, I took over three teams and carefully built an integrated team, which is beginning to perform really well. I believe that the process I went through to gain Chartered Manager status assisted me in achieving this and consequently was of considerable benefit to my organisation.'*
  George Smart, SPO and D/Head of Resettlement, HM Prison Swaleside

To find out more or to request further information please visit our website **www.managers.org.uk/cmgr** or call us on **01536 207429**.

Contents

CHAPTER 02

CHAPTER 03

CHAPTER 04

WHO'S IN CHARGE?   73

CHAPTER 05

WHO'S IN MY TEAM?   93

CHAPTER 06

WILL YOU FINISH IN TIME AND WHERE DID THE MONEY GO?   111

CHAPTER 07

CHAPTER 08

CHAPTER 09

CHAPTER 10

Preface

So, you're involved in a project – and it's either a new experience or one that's taking you near to the boundaries of your know-how or training. You want to get it right – after all, it might lead to bigger things.

The aim of this book is to help you do just that – get it right – and do it well.

Written for people who, like yourself, are either new to managing a project or want to improve your project management skills, it's a book that explains and illustrates the what, why, where, when and how of project management. It will do this in a way that's accessible and easily understood. Rich in diagrams, useful ideas and pointers to appropriate methods and tools, it's *the* book for all of you who wish to develop and learn more about the skills of effective project management. By the time you get to the end of this book you will understand not only what a project is but also what you need to do to successfully plan, manage and control that project. By then, if not before, you should be ready to undertake, with confidence, the process of managing projects successfully.

To get to that point you'll have made your way through the ten chapters of the book. These are arranged in a logical sequence that assumes you've been given a sanctioned project to manage. They will tell you what is, and isn't, a project (Chapter 1); how to organise (Chapter 2), plan (Chapter 3), manage (Chapter 4), and monitor and control your project (Chapter 6) as well as how to assemble your project team (Chapter 5), solve the problems that crop up along the way (Chapter 7), close your project (Chapter 8) and make sure that your project is a success (Chapter 9). But if you haven't been given an already sanctioned project then start off by reading Chapter 1 – to find out about the what, why, where, when and how of projects – and then jump to Chapter 10 – which will tell you how to choose your project and then generate an estimate of your project's cost – and then circle back to the beginning of Chapter 2.

Whichever way you do it, you'll find that each of these chapters:

- starts by telling you what it aims to do and how it will do it
- contains accessible and understandable material that is easily related to your own experience
- finishes with:
  - a summary of the chapter's key points
  - a 'instant tip' that you can take on board to improve your working life.

Above all, it's a book that's aimed at fast-tracking you to where you know a great deal more about projects and project management. When you get there, you'll also be ready to confidently manage a project of your own.

So what are you waiting for?

Acknowledgements

Writing a book like this is not, and can never be, an instant off-the-cuff event. It takes time and patience for the mixture of events, experience and knowledge to come together and then mature. People are always significant in that process. In this instance, special mention should be made of the help given and patience shown by Alison Frecknall, Jill Birch and Harry Scoble at Hodder Education and the counsel and support given, yet again, by my partner Linda Baguley.

01

What is a project?

This chapter is about exploring the project and discovering its nature, characteristics, variety and outcomes. It will also tell you about the Seven Significant Features and Three Dimensions that all projects have. By the end of the chapter, you will have a clear idea about what is, and isn't, a project; what its key characteristics and dimensions are; what a typical project life cycle looks like; how its activities change as it develops, grows and is finally completed and how and why managing a project differs from day-to-day management tasks.

Projects, projects and projects

Projects get talked about quite a lot these days. You'll regularly read about them in your newspapers and magazines and they're often featured on your television and radio. You'll certainly hear about them at work and, at home, you'll probably find your children telling you about their school or homework 'projects'. When you go on the Internet and put the word 'project' into the 'Google' search engine, you'll find you're being offered an amazing five hundred million plus links! Similarly, if you put 'project' into the search box of what's said to be the 'biggest multilingual free-content encyclopedia on the Internet' – Wikipedia – you'll find that you're offered over 140,000 articles.

So, what is this thing we call a 'project' and why is it so popular?

Projects – ancient and modern

At least part of the answer lies in the fact that humankind and projects have been hanging about together for quite a while. The Ark, the Tower of Babel, Stonehenge, the Great Wall of China, Hadrian's Wall and the Pyramids of Egypt are all examples of projects from humankind's past. But history tells us that the creation of such huge structures was a rare, once in a lifetime, event – perhaps because of their size or the enormous resources involved. For example, the construction of Hadrian's Wall in Northern England was probably started in 122AD and took around eight years to complete while the Great Pyramid of Cheops in Egypt took about 20 years to build around 2500BCE. But here and now, in the twenty-first century, things are different. For now projects are not only increasingly present in our lives, they're also here in a greater variety than ever before.

So why has this happened? The answer to this question has two strands to it. The first of these is that we've come to realise how powerful the project is. For it's a mechanism, a process, that:

- is about creating change
- enhances our ability to do things
- enables us to do those things more efficiently and more effectively.

As such, all projects have the potential to be major contributors to the growth, well being and survival of our organisations – whatever their objectives might be and whatever the products or services that they generate. As one project management guru put it 'every project carried out for a commercial organisation is a sub-project to that of achieving its corporate goals'.

The second strand tells us what we already know – that the world in which we work has changed. For now the organisations that we work for have to sell their products in increasingly competitive and volatile worldwide markets. In this hostile and demanding business environment, organisations have to be able to react and respond quickly to the needs of their customers. The project is a proven and effective way of doing just that. It upgrades and focuses the abilities of the organisation and, if used correctly, enables that organisation to respond, effectively and efficiently, to these needs. In short, it enables the organisation to delight its customers.

Projects – great and small

If you think about the projects you've heard about or are familiar with you'll probably come up with recent projects like the preparations for the Beijing 2008 and London 2012 Olympics or the construction of the breathtaking Millau Viaduct that spans 2.5km across a valley in South Western France. Go back a bit further in time and you'll probably turn up the Sydney Opera House, the Channel Tunnel, the 553-metre-high CN tower in Toronto, the 3910-metre-long Akashi-Kaikyo bridge in Japan, Hong Kong's new Chek Lap Kok international airport and China's huge Xiaolangdi dam on the Yellow River. Almost all of these are massive, multi-billion yen, pound or dollar, decade-long mega projects that catch the public eye.

But these aren't the only projects that you'll meet in your life. For there are many, many projects that have much shorter timescales, are far less costly and create outcomes that, whilst important, are not as momentous or huge as those above. It shouldn't take you long to come up with examples – both at home and at work. These will have labels like 'Next Year's Holiday', 'Decorating the Lounge', 'Expanding The Stores', 'Reimaging the Shop', 'Relocating the Office' or 'Installing a Beverage Vending Machine'. Most of these projects will be much, much smaller than the mega projects of the world and, what's just as important, may not even have the label 'project' stuck on them. But they do exist; they are very widespread and very, very abundant. Some estimates put the total world spend on this sort of project at between *50 and 100 times* the total spend on mega projects. When you think about the number of people involved in each of these smaller projects you'll probably find that these are much less than the millions of people involved in the mega projects above. They'll range from the hundreds of people involved when a company relocates down to just two or three people when a new drink vending machine is installed. In fact, most of these mini projects, as you'll see later in this book, involve only two or three people and might only do that on a part-time basis. But, despite this, their ubiquity means that the total number of people involved in small projects exceeds that of the mega projects by several orders of magnitude.

Nevertheless, all of these projects – despite their limited size, scope or ambitions – are important. They are the sorts of project that you probably get involved in as a part of your day-by-day management duties. If you are going to reap the full benefits of their outcomes, you'll need to manage them efficiently and effectively.

Projects – steel and concrete or attitudes and ideas

It's also probable that most of the projects that you're familiar with will have had outcomes that are solid, physical, tangible and touchable. Examples might include the new Wembley Stadium in London, the new office block you pass on the way to work, the new factory that your company has moved into, or the new equipment in your workplace. But these aren't the only sorts of outcomes that projects can have.

For the outcomes of your projects can also be far less tangible or concrete. Examples might be projects that:

- involve gathering information about customers
- result in changed departmental structures
- try to influence the ways in which you or I think or behave.

Examples of this last sort of project – which the theorists would call an 'influencing' project – would include:

- advertising campaigns
- government health campaigns, or
- election campaigns.

These intangible outcome projects might also be about increasing workplace awareness of issues such as quality, waste reduction or customer service – all of which are important and all of which can, and do, contribute to the levels of effectiveness and efficiency of your workplace.

Projects – as a whole

By now, you're probably getting 'tuned in' to both the number and the significance of projects in your life. Your involvement in these projects will vary – with some you'll be watchful but uninvolved while with others you'll have direct and immediate contact. You've also probably picked up the fact that these projects can:

- be concerned with any aspect of your life
- be of any size from small to large
- take days or decades to complete

- involve costs from tens to billions of dollars, yen or pounds
- have outcomes that can be tangible or intangible
- involve any number of people from individuals to nations.

And yet, despite the astonishing range of their outcomes, size, cost and duration, *all* of these projects have a number of common characteristics. This may be difficult for you to accept. How can it be, you might ask, that *all* projects – whether concerned with building a new factory or installing a new vending machine or persuading people to behave in different ways – are basically the same and have a number of very significant features or characteristics in common?

But that is the case – as you will now see.

The Seven Significant Features

The truth is that all projects – whatever their cost, duration or outcome – have a number of features or characteristics in common. These lie at the core of their existence as a project and identifying and understanding them is a major step towards your understanding of the what and how of a project. There are seven of these and they tell us that all projects:

- are about change
- are, in some way, unique
- exist for a limited and defined period of time
- have defined outcomes or targets
- use a variety of resources
- are risky ventures
- involve people.

Let's take a look at these in more detail.

Projects and change

Projects are almost exclusively about change – either knocking down the old or building up the new. This change can be anywhere between large and small and its implications can lie, similarly, anywhere between significant and limited.

Projects and uniqueness

Every project outcome has within it features which are unique to that project. In some projects this uniqueness is considerable. They are singular, one-off, never to be repeated outcomes – like the Pyramids. Other project outcomes, however, possess lesser degrees of uniqueness. For example, the uniqueness of a project outcome of an estate of standard dwelling houses in Brighton, England will be limited to those factors associated with the particular and unique site that they are to be built on. That is to say that while the houses built may be of a standard design and are not unique, the site is unique and will have its own characteristics which will include shape, size, drainage, access, etc.

Projects and time

All projects have defined 'deadlines' or target completion dates. This means that the project has a limited life span – it doesn't go on forever – and will reach a point in time when it is complete. When this point is reached the project will cease to exist. Its management team will disband and move on to other projects or other tasks and the project outcome will be handed over to those who will manage its day-by-day operation. On larger and more complex projects, the project life span can reach out over several years – even decades. But even these projects will reach an end-point and finish.

Projects and outcomes

All projects have well-defined goals, outcomes or sets of desired results. These can be the completion of the building of a house or the publication of a book. These outcomes can also be divided into sub goals or sub tasks which, as you will see later in this book, help the planning, control and management of the project. Often these tasks are interdependent – that is they require other tasks to be completed before they can be completed. But they all must be completed in order to achieve the goal or project outcome.

Projects and resources

One of the singular characteristics of a project is the way in which it uses its resources. For example, a project to build a house will require periods of activity from bricklayers, electricians, carpenters, tilers, plasterers and decorators. These periods of activity will rarely overlap with each other but they will depend upon each other. For example, the decorator cannot start his activities until the carpenter, the plasterer and the tiler have completed their activities. They, in their turn, cannot start their activities until the electrician has completed his or her activities, and so on. The transitory nature of these resources is also present in the equipment needed for the projects – in this case, the diggers, scaffolding, cranes, etc. In a well-managed project these will appear when needed – not before – and leave when their task is complete.

Projects and risk

All projects are about change and that, whichever way you look at it, brings risk with it. Your project – whatever its outcome might be – represents a change. This is a change that's chosen and deliberate – rather than accidental and random – and it also, for most projects, results in a change or changes to:

- the ways in which you or your organisation do things, and/or
- the things that you or your organisation do them with.

But these aren't the only characteristics of your project changes. For they are also sudden – rather than gradual, and significant – rather than trivial. As a result you and your project are exposed to risk, mischance and peril. Later in this chapter and in Chapter 9 you'll see that, in a well-managed project, these risks are identified very early in the project's life cycle. In Chapters 2 and 6 you'll also see that once the project is sanctioned and passes into the 'doing' stages of its life cycle these risks will be examined, monitored and managed. Despite all of this, your project will never be free of risk and its close cousin uncertainty.

Projects and people

Projects are people-centred – they need and demand, whatever their duration or outcomes, the skills and abilities of people in order to create, plan and manage the processes and activities involved. These people and their skills and abilities enable the detail of both the course and content of the project to adapt and change in the face of the vagaries of the 'real' world. While projects share this people-centred characteristic with the day-by-day routine operations which take place in all workplaces, the people demands of projects are different, in both content and magnitude, to those day-to-day routine activities.

Projects and day-by-day activities

When you compare what goes on in a project with what happens in the day-by-day activities of your workplace you'll soon see that these are quite different. For example, a project is temporary and transient while the day-by-day operations of your workplaces are ongoing and repetitive. Take a look at the table below to get a better feel for these differences.

	Project	Day-by-day operations
Timescale	Temporary with defined end and start point	Continuous with no end date
Purpose	To generate change in form of new, specific and unique outcome	To produce identical outcomes or ranges of outcomes repeatedly
Process	One shot, uses transient resources	Ongoing, uses fixed resources
Nature	Unique, temporary and transient	About stability, continuity and repetition

When you've done that you'll realise that projects:
- are different from the other activities that you carry out in your organisation

- must be organised, planned and managed in ways which differ from those that you use in your day-by-day activities.

This means that projects – if they are to be successful – require and demand a different set of approaches and skills in their management. Later in this book you'll find chapters that will take a look at how projects are:

- structured or organised
- managed
- planned
- controlled, and even
- closed.

Projects – a definition

Your exploration of projects and what they do and don't do, should, by now, have brought you to the point where you might be thinking that it would be useful to condense what you've read into a brief and simple definition of a project. But when you start to look at what other people have said and written you'll find that good definitions of what makes a project are a bit thin on the ground. For example, a typical dictionary will tell you that a project is '*a plan or a scheme*' – a definition that doesn't say anything about the project's uniqueness or limited duration. The literature of project management doesn't help much either. For there you'll find material that tells you about '*risk*', '*uncertainty*' and '*steps in to the unknown*' and definitions that speak eloquently of '*human endeavour*', specific outcomes or simply beginnings and ends.

None of these really captures the essence of a project. So, from this point onwards, the definition that this book will use is a simple and straightforward one which tells you that a project is:

A sequence of activities which are:

- **connected**
- **conducted over a limited period of time, and**
- **targeted to generate a unique but well-defined outcome.**

Apply this definition to the examples given earlier in this chapter and you'll see that they all fit – they all display a degree of uniqueness, consist of activities which are connected to each other and have defined outcomes and limited time spans.

Why projects?

Now that you know what a project is you can begin to move on to looking at what you can do with it. For a project is, above all, a change-creating mechanism – one that you can use to achieve any outcome that:

- is unique or one-off in nature
- can be defined
- needs to be created within a specified time period.

It's also a pretty versatile mechanism, one that you can use to do many things. For example, you can use a project to:

- reorganise your company or department
- improve your organisation's performance

- introduce a new way of doing things
- get rid of an old way of doing things
- influence the ways in which people think or feel about something.

Of course, the project isn't the only change-creating mechanism that you'll have as a manager. But it is a powerful and proven one. But, as is so with other instruments of change, the key is in knowing not only *when* to use the project but also, and perhaps more importantly, *how* to use it. In order to ensure that you take the next step on your journey towards that knowledge what you now need to do is to take a look at the key dimensions of projects.

Projects – the key dimensions

It's a common mistake to think about a project only in terms of its outcome. After all, that outcome is probably sitting there looking at you – in the form of the new computer or the rearranged office. But there are other dimensions to this and indeed all projects. You might ask, for example, questions about:

- how long did the rearrangement take?
- how much did it cost?
- were the furniture and desks moved to the positions that you had chosen?
- did the rearrangement achieve what you wanted it to?

If you think about it you'll soon begin to see that projects have three dimensions:

- the nature of the outcomes or performance
- the time taken or needed to achieve that performance
- the costs of all the resources used in the project.

It will also soon become clear to you that these dimensions do not stand alone. You cannot, for example, change the cost of a project without taking into account the effect that has upon both the project outcome and its duration.

In short, these dimensions are inter-related and complementary. For example, if you are running out of time to complete a project by the due date or time, you could speed things up in one of two ways:

● by taking on extra labour
● by doing less than you had planned to do.

But both of these actions will have consequences. Taking on extra labour will certainly increase the cost of the project. The other alternative of doing less will mean that you spend less but fail to achieve your planned outcome. In another situation, an unplanned and late increase in the scope of the project will require increases in both time and money to compensate. All three of these dimensions of the project can and do exert a significant influence on the ways in which you manage your project. You must take them into account when you define, manage, plan, monitor and control a project. Figure 1.1 shows the dynamic interconnectedness of these dimensions.

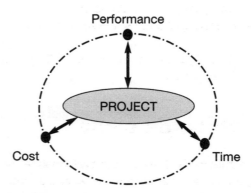

Figure 1.1: The three dimensions of projects

As one of these dimensions moves or changes it affects the other two – almost as if they are connected by bits of elastic.

These key dimensions are in all projects, large or small. Let's look at a project to build a large house and see if we can put more detail to each of these key dimensions:

- **outcome:** number and size of rooms, shape, facilities, capacity, for example four bed, two bath timber frame ranch house with patio, outdoor swimming pool and barbecue decorated in specified finishes and colours
- **cost:** £500,000
- **duration:** to be ready for occupation by 1 December 2020.

If you change any of the details of any one of these dimensions it will have an effect upon the other two. If, for example, you add another bedroom it will increase both the cost and the duration.

These three dimensions of Time, Cost, and Outcome are *the* key dimensions for all projects. Whatever the size or nature of the project, they must be:

- clearly defined at the beginning of the project
- monitored throughout its duration
- carefully managed and controlled at all times.

Indeed, failing to do this can, as you'll see in Chapter 9, only have one result – a failed project!

The project life cycle

Projects have a life cycle. They start, grow from small beginnings to become larger and then mature and ultimately die. You'll be familiar with this pattern of growth and decline – you'll have seen and experienced these changes not only in your own life but also in the lives of your family pets and the flowers and plants that you grow in your garden. Apply it to the project and you'll find the following stages in its life cycle:

Conception

This is the stage in which the project is identified, its feasibility reviewed and initial estimates of cost generated as are the initial definitions of performance and time required. By the end of this stage, a decision as to whether to proceed with the project will be taken. A 'Yes' decision leads to the next stage of growth while a 'No' decision leads to the death of the project. Many embryonic projects die at this stage and Chapter 10 describes how this choice is made.

Birth and development

This is the stage in which the detailed design of the project outcome is developed and decisions are taken about who will do what and when. Cost and time estimates are also refined. This stage involves a relatively low, though accelerating, pace of activity.

Adulthood

Here the planned work takes place. The stage with the highest activity rate, it also requires the use of effective monitoring, control and forecasting procedures. These should tell the project manager about what:

- has or hasn't been done or spent
- ought to have been done or spent
- will need to be done or spent in the future.

The project will reach completion at the end of this stage and the outcome will be handed over to those who will use it.

Old age and termination

In this, the final stage, the review and audit of the project and the break up of the project team take place. The pace of activities falls and finally stops.

These life cycle stages are illustrated in Figure 1.2. You'll have noticed that throughout this cycle not only does what is done change – the rates at which things are done also change. This means that the demands and needs for resources or effort of each of the life cycle stages will be different from each other and will wax and wane within each stage. For almost all projects, large or small, it's the adulthood stage, with its focus on getting things done, that displays the peaks of resource demands.

Managing and projects

Managing is never easy. It's rather like a juggling act – you struggle to balance the differing needs of the task, the organisation, the customer and your staff; needs that are often in conflict with each other or pulling in opposite directions. In your day-by-day operations you can trade off the dimensions of time, performance and cost in order to prevent one of these from falling below the required levels or standards. But, in the project, things are different. Your project has, for example, a finite and fixed time scale for its completion. As a result, your freedom as a project manager to trade

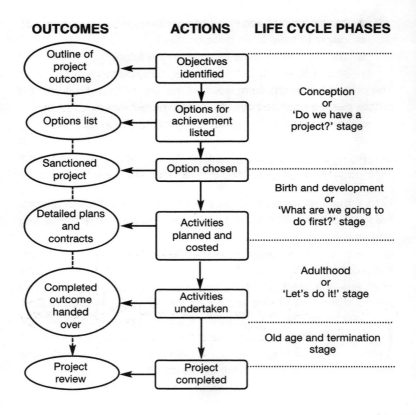

OUTCOMES **ACTIONS** **LIFE CYCLE PHASES**

OUTCOMES	ACTIONS	LIFE CYCLE PHASES
Outline of project outcome	Objectives identified	
Options list	Options for achievement listed	Conception or 'Do we have a project?' stage
Sanctioned project	Option chosen	
Detailed plans and contracts	Activities planned and costed	Birth and development or 'What are we going to do first?' stage
Completed outcome handed over	Activities undertaken	Adulthood or 'Let's do it!' stage
Project review	Project completed	Old age and termination stage

Figure 1.2: Project life cycle

off time against money, performance or even quality is limited, sometimes even non-existent. Being a project manager is different from being a day-by-day manager. You've already seen that projects are very different from day-by-day tasks and as a result they must be organised, planned and managed in ways that are different from those that you use in your day-by-day activities. Being a project manager requires different attitudes and a different skill set. All of these are deployed in a conversion process; one that takes the inputs of:

- **information** – about timescales, cost, performance, quality and the client
- **people** – with their skills, needs, experience and abilities
- **resources** – of materials, equipment, money and time.

It's also a process that, more importantly, converts these inputs into a specific and unique outcome as illustrated in Figure 1.3.

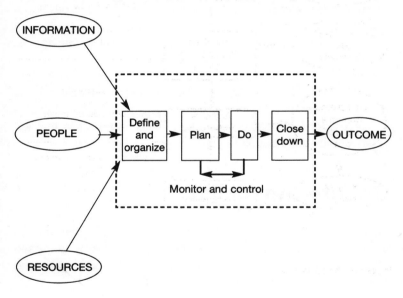

Figure 1.3: The project process

But this project management isn't carried out in a vacuum. As a project manager, you'll have to cope with the pulls and pressures of several groups of people – the client, the other people and organisations who have a stake or interest in the project and, last but not least, the project team. You'll have to make sure that the original integrity of the project is maintained – despite the conflicts, arguments and rivalries which arise between these groups and the risks and problems that spring up like toadstools along the project's journey to completion. You'll need to lead and motivate your team of project staff – staff who will only be members of that team for the duration of the project and who may have been 'borrowed' from other departments or functions.

To do all of this and manage what are often considerable but fluctuating levels of resources means that you'll need to develop a rare mix of skills and abilities.

Managing a project is not an easy task. The project manager is, as one project guru tells us, the chief executive officer of the temporary organisation that exists solely to create the project outcome. This role, as you'll see in the following chapters, is not one for the faint hearted. Do it well, though, and you'll find that you've acquired and developed a package of skills and abilities that will make a major contribution to your career.

Chapter checklist

Well done! You've covered quite a lot of ground in this chapter. Use the list below to check out where you've got to. If you've missed something or didn't understand it go back to the page given and read it through again.

- The project is a very common way of creating change (page 2).
- Projects can:
  - be large or small (page 3)
  - have a wide range of outcomes both, tangible and intangible (page 4)

- involve any number of people (page 4)
- have life spans of days, years or decades (page 4).
- All projects:
  - have outcomes that are, to greater or lesser degrees, unique (page 7)
  - are concerned with change (page 7)
  - have defined outcomes and endpoints (page 8)
  - use a variety of transitory resources (page 8)
  - are risky ventures (page 9)
  - involve people (page 9).
- Managing a project is different from managing day-by-day tasks (page 10).
- A project can be defined as: a sequence of connected activities which take place over a limited period of time and are targeted to generate a unique but well-defined outcome (page 12).
- The key dimensions of a project are:
  - outcome
  - cost
  - time (page 13).
- Project life cycles have the stages of:
  - conception (page 16)
  - birth and development (page 16)
  - adulthood (page 16)
  - old age and termination (page 17).
- These stages have different rates of activity and resource demands (page 17).
- Project management is a conversion process that:
  - takes in: information, people and resources (page 19)
  - converts them into a specific and unique outcome (page 19)
  - requires a rare set of skills (page 20).

INSTANT TIP

Project success comes when you keep the three project dimensions of time, cost and outcome on track.

02

How do you organise your project?

Getting organised, and staying that way, is a vital part of managing a project. In this chapter you'll remind yourself about what being organised involves and the benefits that come with it. You'll also look at the different sorts of project organisation that exist and their pros and cons together with the need for project procedures and specifications. By the end of the chapter you'll be able to decide not only what sort of organisation will be best for your project but also what the forms, procedures and specifications of your project will look like.

O is for organising

History tells us that human beings have been organising for a long time. First, there were tribes; then, there were religions and then, there were nations – all of which came about because people wanted to be organised. Here, in the twenty-first century, things aren't really that different. We organise ourselves in all sorts of ways and into all sorts of groups both at work and at home. When you do that it means that you can:

- do things that you couldn't do on your own
- get benefits from being a member of a group or an organisation
- get the protection that can come from being in that group or organisation.

As an individual, being organised means that you:

- use what time you have more effectively
- have more time to spend on achieving your goals
- are more efficient – you achieve more in less time
- have more control over what you do and don't do
- have reduced stress, frustration and anxiety levels.

However, being organised does have a down side. For when you are organised you:

- are less able to respond spontaneously to those events that need you to do that
- try to solve problems logically or linearly (see Chapter 7) when less logical or more creative and intuitive ways of doing this might have worked better
- are less open to those useful 'accidental' or serendipitous discoveries or events that can give you your best results
- will often have to consult those around you before taking a decision or doing something
- will have to obey the 'rules' of the organisation.

Nevertheless being organised – whatever its pros and cons might be – is a fact of life here in the twenty-first century; one that's here to stay. But that's not all, for this sequence or event of becoming organised has led to the creation of the dominant social structure of our modern society – the organisation. These organisations – which are systems of rules, procedures and principles – are the homes of our projects.

Projects and organisations

If you stand a project and an organisation side by side you'll soon see that they seem to have a lot in common. For they both:

- have objectives or targets
- are people-centred
- have leaders
- are structured
- use systems and procedures.

But there are differences. These begin to emerge when you look in more detail at things like the time horizons, objectives and outcomes of the organisation and the project.

	Organisations	Projects
Time horizon	Long term and continual	Defined and limited
Objectives	Continual survival	Completion, termination
Outcomes	Replicas or hybrids	Unique, one-off

What this table tells you is that the organisation is here for the long run – unlike the project, which is a transitory, almost ephemeral event. The organisation's objective – continual survival – is almost the exact opposite of the project's objective of completion and termination. Their outcomes also differ with the organisation generating replicas or hybrids modified by incremental changes and the project creating a unique, one-off, outcome.

But these differences don't mean that the organisation and the project are incompatible or can't work together. You saw in

Chapter 1 that the project is a change-creating mechanism. The power and flexibility of the project means that it can be used by all organisations. It can be used, for example, to create the changes needed to ensure that an organisation's regular day-by-day activities are carried out efficiently and effectively. It can also be used to change the structure of that organisation, moving it into a form that is even more responsive to the tides and challenges of today's global marketplace.

Organising projects – the overview

Before you look at the how and why of organising your project it's worth stepping back and reminding yourself about the key characteristics of all your projects. As you saw in Chapter 1, these are that projects:

- have unique outcomes
- are concerned with change
- take place over a limited and defined period of time
- use a variety of transitory resources.

If you are going to manage your project successfully then you'll need to organise, structure and manage it in ways that answer the needs of:

- the client organisation
- the project
- the project team.

These needs are often in conflict and your project organisation must be strong and robust to cope with this. It must also be flexible, responsive and focused on problem solving so that it can bring about the pragmatic and practical compromises, between those conflicting needs, that will lead to project success.

The nature of your project organisation will also be influenced by a wide range of other factors including the project's:

- duration – as in days or decades
- cost – as in hundreds or billions of pounds or euros
- complexity – as in ten or 30,000 interconnected activities
- importance to the client – as in 'vital to survival' or 'just another project'
- importance to project team – as in 'we are the greatest' or 'done that, got the t-shirt'
- innovative nature – as in 'rocket to Jupiter' or 'just another house'.

If your project is going to cope with all of these influences and complexity then it must be organised well and in a way that ensures that it:

- is compatible with the client organisation
- provides an effective framework for all of the project's activities.

Project organisations – the choices

Let's begin your exploration of the choices available to you when you organise your project by taking a brief look at two very different projects in the same organisation.

The first of these is a low cost, short duration project with the objective of introducing a computer system for recording client data and till management in a hairdressing salon. The system is being gradually introduced across a chain of salons using computers and software that are well proven, having been used successfully in a considerable number of similar locations. However, keeping these records on a computer is a new and challenging task for the management and staff of this particular salon. They are, however, aware of the importance of the project and are motivated to 'make it work'. If this project is going to be successful then it must be organised in a way that primarily answers the needs of these people. As a result the organisation for this project will have:

- a structure that reflects that of the salon
- a project leader or manager who works in the salon
- team members from the salon and the hardware/ software suppliers
- management and control systems that are integrated into those already used in the salon.

With a project organisation like this the salon staff will be involved, in one way or another, in all of the phases of the project. This involvement will start by answering questions like 'where do we put the computer?' and finish with a final handover test. While doing this they will be able to watch and learn, draw on the knowledge of the suppliers and see ways of using the training that they will have been given.

The second project is sited in the head office of the salon chain and is focused on the introduction of a high cost, complex, integrated computer driven management information system (MIS). This will integrate, in real time, the information that will become available when all of the salons in the chain have successfully completed their individual client data projects. Success in a project like this, which will have a medium–long time span and is technically innovative, will require:

- high levels of skill in planning and managing innovative large projects
- MIS project experience.

The needs of the project will be dominant here and will result in a project organisation that will have:

- a project team which is separate from the company head office organisation
- its own management and control systems.

With a project organisation like this head office staff will have limited involvement in the project until the final handover test. But they will liaise with the project team and be trained in the new hardware and software that the project creates.

These two very different projects have given you a glimpse of the different ways in which projects can be organised.

Project organisation – the details

You will have noticed that the project organisations in the above examples differed by virtue of:

- which set of needs – client , project or project team – was dominant
- the degree of separation between the project organisation and the client organisation.

In the salon project the client needs were dominant and the separation of the project organisation and the client organisation was limited, almost negligible. In the head office project, however, the project needs were dominant and the project organisation–client organisation separation was significant and substantial. These two factors – whose needs dominate and the degree of separation – are critical when it comes to identifying and describing the three main types of project organisation. Let's look at each of these in turn.

Client Focus organisation

In this type of project organisation, it's the needs of the client that dominate and, as a result, the project organisation and client organisation are very close. So close, in fact, that the project organisation is a part of or integrated into the client organisation. The project is staffed – often, but not always, on a part-time basis – by people who work for that client organisation. This project team will use office space and other facilities that exist within the client organisation. As a result this team can easily tap into and use the resources, functional skills and expertise contained in that client organisation. It also means that the project's procedures and systems will be compatible with, if not the same as, the procedures and systems used by the client and that the skill, knowledge and experience gained by project team members is retained within the client organisation.

But all of this closeness and compatibility does have a down side. For in a project with a client focus organisation:

- the day-to-day needs of the client organisation can dominate decisions about the 'who-has-what-and-when' of resources
- the allegiances of project team members are to their functional 'home' – rather than the project or project team
- authority of the project manager can be limited and beset by organisational 'politics'.

The location of the project within the client organisation will, of course, be strongly influenced by the nature of the project outcome. For example, a project with an outcome of a new piece of production equipment will be placed under the overall control and supervision of the Production Department, while a project that aims to raise employee awareness of quality will find a home in the Quality Department.

Project Focus organisation

In this type of project organisation, it's the project needs that dominate and the project organisation and the client organisation stand well clear of each other. The project team exists as a separate and self-contained organisational unit, with its own resources, staff, offices, etc. This team communicates with the client organisation by means of regular progress reports. These are usually delivered at project progress meetings attended by senior management from the client organisation.

The advantages of this sort of project organisation include:

- project team with a clear stand-alone identity
- project team members are committed to the project
- project manager has full control of the project
- speedy problem solving and decision taking are focused on project needs.

Its disadvantages include:

- duplication of staff if several projects are in progress within the same organisation
- potential for incompatibility in systems and procedures between project and client organisations
- loss of skill and knowledge when project ends and project team members disperse.

Matrix organisation

This type of project organisation tries to be a compromise between the extremes of the client and project focus organisations. In its simplest form the project manager – who has a full-time role –

draws personnel from each of the client organisation's functional departments. Its advantages include:

- ease of access to client organisation people
- compatibility between systems and procedures

and its disadvantages reflect the fact that:

- team members have two bosses – project manager and functional manager
- stability of the balance of power between project manager and functional managers can be fragile
- project manager takes project administration decisions while functional managers control technical decisions.

The success or failure of this type of project organisation has also been observed to be unduly dependent upon the personality and skills of the project manager.

If you take a look at the following table it will give you an idea of some of the characteristics of these different types of project organisation.

	Client Focus	**Matrix**	**Project Focus**
Project Manager authority level	Low	Low/medium	High
% of project staff full-time	nil	15–60	85–100
Project Manager role	Part time	Full time	Full time

Your project organisation

Choosing the 'right' sort of organisation for your project is a key step towards success for your project. Get it right and you'll have a good framework for your planning, monitoring and control activities as well as your management of the project. Get it wrong and you'll be fighting an increasingly difficult and losing battle throughout the lifetime of the project. To choose the right organisation for your project you'll need to:

● find out and understand what worked, or didn't work, on past projects
● understand the client organisation's skills, experience, and equipment
● be aware of the project's outcomes, risks, cost, duration and special technology needs
● decide what will work for you.

So where do you start?

The first thing that you must do is to get information about your project. This information needs to be clear, specific, numerate and accurate. Sweeping generalisations are not enough. So if your project is about upgrading your desktop computer, you'll need to have information about the processor speed, RAM size, hard disk capacity, operating system and flat screen size of the desired outcome. You'll also need to answer questions about training needs and environmental factors associated with the new computer. Earlier in this chapter you saw that a range of factors, such as the project's duration, cost, complexity, importance and level of innovation can influence the project organisation that you choose. Now you have to be much more detailed and specific. So take a look at and use the checklist in Figure 2.1.

Treat every heading as a question and fill in the information that you have. If you don't have any leave a blank.

Project Outcome:

Planned project start date : / /   Finish date: / /
Planned project duration:

Planned project budget:
Accuracy of estimate:

Special/new technology:
Special knowledge needs:

Project Risk Factor on scale 0–10 (0 = low risk, 10 = very high risk):

Importance of project to client organisation on scale 0–10 (0 = another routine project, 10 = vital to organisation survival):

Figure 2.1: Project information checklist

Once you've filled in this checklist and have satisfied yourself that it contains the best information that is currently available, then you're ready to move on to the next step. This involves using the information on the Project Organisation Selection Flowchart (in Figure 2.2). This should give you a strong indication as to what sort of organisation is right for your project. But if you find that your accumulated points total is near the boundary between one type of organisation and another then:

- go back and check your information
- find out how previous projects in your organisation were organised and whether they worked and last, but not least,
- use your judgement.

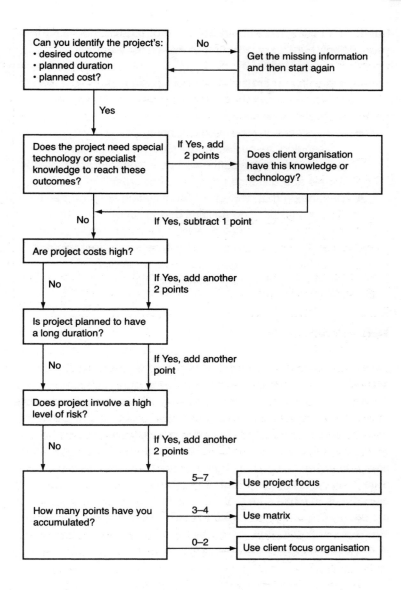

Figure 2.2: Project organisation selection flowchart

But if you're still unsure about what sort of organisation is right for your project, here's some further guidance for you:

- projects that are small, short in duration and have low costs are usually best handled by a client focus type project organisation
- projects that involve new technology can be very challenging, resource hungry and risky. A project focus type project organisation that uses subcontractors keeps all this at a distance from the client organisation
- pretending that your client organisation has got the functional skills and abilities that the project needs – when it really hasn't – is a recipe for disaster. A project focus organisation or a matrix type project organisation can effectively control, monitor and manage the subcontractors that you'll need to use.

Review

Let's just take a look at where you've got to. Now, you can recognise what is and isn't a project, identify the seven significant features and three dimensions of your project and know about and understand its life cycle. You're also able to choose the type of project organisation that you feel is going to be the best one for your project.

So what's next and where do you go now? The answer is that now you have to begin to decide the detail of the process of organising your project. But this won't be a simple task. Its objective is to make sure that every thing that happens inside your project – its internal processes – is organised and carried out effectively and efficiently. To make sure that happens you're going to need two things:

1. the organising skills that you use in your day-by-day management role
2. a set of the basic procedures and documents.

What documents?

These procedures and documents are important. Get them right and they will describe and define:

- the Time, Cost and Outcome dimensions of your project
- how you are going manage, monitor and control your project.

Get them wrong and you'll finish up with a pile of useless bureaucratic paperwork that doesn't get used and will only add to the confusion of a failing project.

A basic but workable set of these documents will include the following:

Project Specification or Project Initiation Document (PID)

In its simplest form this should tell you about the project's:

- name or title and reference number (if any)
- justification, objectives and deliverables
- expenditure and timetable
- organisation and responsibilities.

It can also, when relevant, identify the quality control and risk evaluation procedures that will be used throughout the project. You'll see in Chapter 10 that this sort of document is also used in the pre-sanction or conception stage of a project's life cycle when it's extended so that it can contain the information required for the process of choosing which project is sanctioned. However, once a project is approved or sanctioned, this document then acts as a definition of the project and a baseline against which project progress is assessed and requested changes assessed. See Figure 2.3 for a simple version of this form.

Project roles and responsibilities

It's important that you define the 'who-does-what' of the project process. In it's fullest form this document should cover all the members of the project team and should define:

- what role they have
- the responsibilities and duties of that role
- reporting and authority aspects.

On smaller projects this document can take the form of a simple chart as is shown in Figure 2.4.

Project change control

As the project progresses you'll soon find that, despite all your efforts, you become beset with requests to modify or change the original project definition contained in the Project Specification Document. These must be resisted and controlled at all costs.

On being asked for a change, you, as project manager, must insist on a change request form being completed by someone in authority. This will enable you to evaluate:

- the impact of the change
- any increase in cost and/or time.

Changes should only be approved by senior management. Figure 2.5 is an example of a simple change control form.

Project Specification Form	
Project title:	Reference no.:
Project objectives:	
Project deliverables:	
Project manager:	Tel no.:
Project sponsor:	Tel no.:
Start date:	Completion date:
Capital sanctioned:	Estimate ref no.:
Project team:	Client contacts:
Approved by: Project manager:	Date:
Project sponsor:	Date:

Figure 2.3: Project specification form

TASK AREA	Project Manager	Mechanical Engineer	Civil Engineer	Electrical Engineer	Instrument Engineer	Process Design Engineer
Flowsheet design	◆	■		■	❖	●
Plant layout	◆	●	❖	■	■	■
Piping design	◆	●	■		❖	■
Instrumentation	◆			■	●	❖
Power supply	◆			●	■	

Key:
  ● Responsible
  ◆ Approval
  ■ Notified
  ❖ Support

Figure 2.4: Project role responsibility chart

Project Change Request	
Number:	Date:
Approved/Rejected/Held	
Proposed change:	
Reasons for change:	
Areas affected:	
Documents and drawing affected:	
Requested by:	Evaluated by:
Date:	Date:

Figure 2.5: Project change control form

Milestone monitoring

You'll see in Chapter 3 that a project milestone is a significant point in the project. It's usually a point on the project's 'critical path' – the sequence of activities that determines the earliest point in time at which the project will finish. So reaching a project milestone is just like reaching a milestone on a road – it tells you how far you've come and how far you've yet to go. The milestone-monitoring document is a simple way of monitoring project progress (see Figure 2.6).

Milestone no.	Scheduled date	Anticipated date	Achieved date	Notes
4	25 Oct.		24 Oct.	Completed ahead of schedule
5	13 Dec.	15 Dec.	–	Material delivery delay anticipated

Figure 2.6: Milestone report form

Risk management

You've already seen in Chapter 1 that all projects are risky ventures. Later in this book, in Chapter 9, you'll see how the risks of your project can be identified and reduced. But the remaining risks still need to be monitored and controlled and Figure 2.7 will help you to do that.

Risk ID no.	Risk description	Control measure	Person responsible	Completion date

Figure 2.7: Risk control form

Budget and cost control

It's important – as you'll see in Chapter 6 – that your project spend is monitored and controlled. The way that you do this and the accounting conventions and procedures that you'll use will, to a degree, depend upon how close your project organisation is to the client organisation. If you've chosen to use a Client Focus or Matrix type project organisation then your cost control procedures will need to be compatible with, if not identical to, those of your client. If you've chosen a Project Focus organisation then these procedures can be whatever you choose them to be – providing they are effective.

Procedures and specifications

So where will you find these and the other documents that you'll need for your project?

The first place to look is within your own organisation. If you're lucky, you'll find that these documents or the pro forma blanks for them are already there, in an existing Manual of Project

Organisation and Procedures. But if you're unlucky and this manual doesn't exist then the next step in your search is to find out what documentation was used on previous projects. Take care with what you find though because being used before doesn't necessarily mean that it will be of use or value to you.

But even if this fails there are, on the Internet and in various publications, a number of examples of forms and documents that you can use on your project. Sources will include RIBA's 'Plan of Work', Australia's HIA Quality Management and Systems, America's standards for Software Project Management (IEEE), Project Management (AIA) and Cost Engineering and Project Management (ANSI) and the British Standards Guide to Project Management (BS6079) and Use of Network Techniques in Project Management (BS6046).

Wherever you get your project documentation from you need to review it before you start to use it for real. Use the Checklist below to do that.

Project Documentation Checklist

	Yes	No
Does your Project Specification state:		
• what the project has undertaken to supply?	☐	☐
• when it is to be supplied by?	☐	☐
• where it is to be supplied?	☐	☐
• at what cost?	☐	☐
Does your Project Role Responsibility Chart state:		
• what project team roles are to be carried out?	☐	☐
• what the responsibilities of those roles are?	☐	☐
• who has been appointed to those roles?	☐	☐
Does your Project Change request form ask for?		
• a definition of and reason for proposed change?	☐	☐
• what's affected by this proposed change?	☐	☐

Does your Risk Control form tell you:	Yes	No
• what the risk is?	☐	☐
• how that is going to be controlled?	☐	☐
Does your Milestone report form tell you:		
• when a milestone should have been completed?	☐	☐
• when it was completed?	☐	☐

Key: If you have more than two 'nos' then you need to review and change your project documentation – before you have a problem!

Chapter checklist

That's another step taken on the road that will lead to you being an effective project manager. Use the list below to check out where you've got to. If you've missed something or didn't understand it go back to the page given and read it through again.

- Being organised is important (page 24).
- Projects and organisations have a lot in common but are also different in significant ways (page 25).
- Projects need to be organised and the organisation of your project needs to be compatible with the client organisation and provide an effective framework for all of the project's activities (page 27).
- Choosing the right organisation for your project is important and the alternatives are: Client focus organisation (page 30); Project focus organisation (page 31) and Matrix organisation (page 31).
- To choose the right organisation for your project you need to:
  - find out and understand what worked, or didn't work, on past projects

- understand the client organisation's skills, experience, and equipment
- be aware of the project's outcomes, risks, cost, duration and special technology needs
- decide what will work for you (page 33).
- Then you need to generate:
  - a project specification (page 37)
  - role descriptions and responsibility charts (page 38)
  - procedures for change control (page 41) and milestone and risk management (page 42).

INSTANT TIP

Effective organisation is crucial to the successful delivery of projects on time, to budget and specification.

03

Do you have a plan?

Plans and projects are close companions. If fact, you could say – as the old song does – that 'you can't have one without the other'. In this chapter you'll look at why planning your project is so important and examine the principles, steps and stages of the process that you'll use to do that planning. By the end of the chapter you'll know and understand a lot more about planning, planning tools such as Gantt charts, Activity on Arrow and Activity on Node networks and how you can get computers to help you to plan your project.

P is for planning

Planning is something that we all do. Some of us do it well and others of us do it badly; some plan with meticulous attention to detail, others plan with 'broad-brush' strokes. But we all do it – particularly when we want to create a future event or happening. In its most basic form, this planning is a thought process; an internal 'what-shall-we-do-next?' sequence of ideas that takes us from where we are to where we want to be. It can also, of course, be more complex and sophisticated than that. It can, for example, involve documents, diagrams and meetings; all aimed at deciding and defining the issues to be addressed, the objectives to be met, and the tactics and strategies to be followed.

However you do it, the outcome is a plan. This plan is a statement of intent; it's about how we are going to get from one situation or set of circumstances to another. While often about moving from a present or almost certain near future situation towards one or more future and less certain objectives or goals, plans can also be about moving from one uncertain or possible future situation to another just as uncertain situation.

Plans can also be off-the-cuff and informal or structured and formal. They spring into existence because of the thoughts and actions of both individuals and groups of people. They can be about the achievement of our personal goals and desires or concerned with projects or missions of all sorts; such as diplomatic missions, economic development plans, military campaigns or simply the conduct of business.

The less formal the plan, the more likely it is to remain as an abstract idea – even during its implementation. However, more formal plans – such as those used in the world of work – are likely to be written down, drawn up and recorded in a form that can be stored and sent to other people. Doing this, as you will see later in this chapter, helps us to communicate with each other during the course of the plan's execution.

Planning and projects

In Chapter 1 you saw that all projects have three key dimensions – Time, Cost and Performance. You also saw that projects have well-defined outcomes or targets and exist for a limited and defined period of time. All of this should give you a pretty broad hint as to why it is that the plan is so important to a project. For the project plan is the mechanism that you use to convert the outcomes of the project from statements of intent to the concrete reality of achieved objectives. Without a plan your project would be like an untethered kite – driven far and wide, high and low by the winds of chance and circumstance. But with a plan – particularly a good one – you are able to reach out to guide and control the passage of your project from intention to substance and from proposal to reality. But if your project plan is going to do that for you then it must:

- contain enough detail to make it meaningful and usable but not so much detail that it becomes unnecessarily complicated
- be easily understood by all who use it
- be easy to change, update and revise
- be easy to use to monitor project progress and as a means of communication.

But that's not all that you need from your project plan.

A good plan will not only have all these characteristics, it will also be able to do something else. It will draw in and act as a focusing 'lens' for the skills, abilities and energy of the people who, as you saw in Chapter 1, are one of the key Seven Significant Features of all projects. Start your project by creating a plan that can do all of this and then you're more than halfway towards success. Fail to do that – and find yourself with a plan that's difficult to understand or full of irrelevant detail or slow and difficult to update – then you've not only got a problem; you've also got a failing project!

So let's get started on your good plan!

In the beginning

In Chapter 2 you saw that the Project Specification or Project Initiation Document (PID) became, after the project has been sanctioned, a baseline against which project progress and any requested changes are assessed.

But that's not all that it becomes. This document also provides you with a starting point for the creation of your project plan. It tells you about the project's goals, objectives, timescale and budgeted cost. But in order to convert these into a plan you'll also have to know or find the answers to questions such as:

- what actions are needed to reach those goals and objectives within the given time span and at the budgeted cost?
- when do these actions need to start and finish?
- who will carry out these actions?
- what equipment, tools and materials are needed?

The answers to these questions contain the details of the future actions of your project. These details will, of course, be particular to your project but for all projects the document that contains them is called a Work Breakdown Schedule (WBS). A simple example, for a small domestic project that may be familiar to some of you, is given in Figure 3.1.

On larger projects, life is often more complicated and your WBS will have several levels – each with ascending degrees of detail. The level of detail contained in your WBS is important. Too much and you'll finish with a project plan that's unmanageable – because it's far too detailed. Too little and you'll finish up with a project plan that is so broad-brush that it serves little purpose. Here are some general guidelines to help you decide the level of detail and the activities that are right for your WBS:

Project goals and objectives: To redecorate or remodel a small bedroom

Actions needed:
- remove furniture, curtains and light shades
- protect carpet
- strip off existing wallpaper and remove waste
- fill any wall damage and sand down
- remove old paint from woodwork and remove waste
- repair defect and sand down woodwork
- vacuum to remove dust
- wash down ceiling
- paint ceiling
- prime, undercoat and topcoat paint woodwork
- paper walls
- clean up waste and remove carpet protection
- replace light shades, furniture and curtains

Completion date: 10 December

Duration: four days (two weekends)

Actions by: Phil and Linda Baguley

Equipment, tools and material needed:

Paint brushes	Paint roller	Paint remover and scrapers
Wallpaper scrapers	Filler	Sandpaper
Step ladder	Wallpaper adhesive and brush	
Pasting table	Scissors, measure and plumb line	
Plastic sheets	Emulsion paint for ceiling	
Primer, undercoat and gloss paint for woodwork		
Wallpaper brush	Vacuum cleaner	Wallpaper
Bucket, cloths and detergent		Plastic waste bags
Brush cleaner		

Figure 3.1: Work breakdown schedule for small project

- Don't show a task as a separate activity if its duration is less than 5 per cent of the total project duration but remember that, irrespective of project total duration, there will always be short duration activities that are so important that they must be included in your WBS and project plan – such as getting planning permission or authorisation to proceed.
- Relate the units of your plan and the activity detail to the overall project duration. For example:

Overall duration	Plan timescale units	Exclude as solo activity if less than
weeks	day	$1/2$ day
months	day	1 day
years	week	1 week

- Include activities that, when complete, signal a shift or transfer of responsibility – such as placing purchase orders with supplier, completion of material deliveries or handover of completed packages.

Once you've generated your WBS you will begin to see the way that the three project dimensions – Time, Cost and Performance – interact with and influence each other. For example, a limited budget for the project in Figure 3.1 would influence the quality of wallpaper that you buy and might also persuade you to paint over the existing wood finish – thus eliminating the cost of primer, undercoat, paint remover and scrapers as well as reducing the time needed to complete the woodwork painting.

You'll also need to know if there are any of these actions that cannot be started until other actions are finished. In the jargon of project planning this is called 'interdependency'. On this project there are several of these as shown in Figure 3.2.

Action no.	Can only be completed after Action no.
1. Remove furniture, curtains and light shades	–
2. Protect carpet	1
3. Strip off existing wallpaper and remove waste	2
4. Fill any wall damage and sand down	3
5. Remove old paint from woodwork and remove waste	3
6. Repair defects and sand down woodwork	5
7. Vacuum to remove dust	4 and 6
8. Wash down ceiling	2
9. Paint ceiling	8 and 7
10. Prime, undercoat and topcoat paint woodwork	5 and 7
11. Paper walls	4, 9 and 10
12. Clean up waste and remove carpet protection	11
13. Replace light shades, furniture and curtains	12

Figure 3.2: Action interdependency table

This example tells you that, because there are two people on the project, it might be possible for Action 5 to be carried out at the same time as Action 4 and for Action 8 to be carried out at any time after Action 2 completion. As a result, Actions 4 and 5 and Actions 8, 3, 4, 5, 6 and 7 could be called parallel activities or activities that can be carried out at the same time. But before you can be sure that this is possible you need to know how long each of these activities will take.

Estimating duration of an activity has been described as a mixture of science, experience and intuition. There are a number of sources for the information that you need to do this well. On this project, paint manufacturers (touch dry after 3 hours, recoat after 8 hours), people who have done it before (friends, family or books) and your own experience (what did we do last time?) will all help the accuracy of your activity duration estimation. Another way around this uncertainty is to use the following formula:

Expected duration = (a + 4m+b)/6
Where a = optimistic duration
       b = pessimistic duration
and   m = most likely duration

However, when a project takes you beyond the boundaries of your prior experience or easily accessible information, then it's time to get more professional help.

Once you've got your activity duration estimate information together then you'll be ready to take the next step – generating the first draft of your plan. But before you do that you need to remember that not only does your plan act as a record of your intentions, it also acts as a way of presenting these intentions and your decisions about them to the project team, the client and the other people and organisations who have an interest in the project.

Most information is best presented in a visual form – and the project plan is no exception. There are several visual conventions for project plans and we will look at three of the most popular of these:

- Gantt chart
- Activity on Arrow networks
- Precedence networks.

Bars and charts

One of the oldest and simplest forms of the project plan is the bar chart or Gantt chart. An American engineer and management consultant called Henry L. Gantt developed this in the early part of the twentieth century. A follower of F.W. Taylor's 'Scientific Management' approach, Gantt made many contributions to manufacturing management including the 'task and bonus' system of wage payment and methods of measuring worker efficiency and productivity. Gantt charts were employed on many major American early twentieth-century infrastructure projects including the Hoover Dam and Interstate highway system. Despite its age the Gantt chart is still an important and popular tool in twenty-first century project management.

The Gantt or bar chart has:

- a horizontal timescale
- a vertical list of activities
- a horizontal line or bar for each activity.

The lengths of these horizontal bars are proportional to the time needed to complete the activity (see Figure 3.3).

The Gantt chart, with its timescale base and visual representation of activity duration and completion, gives you a clear and easily understandable picture of the project. It's also one that you can use to communicate with others. It also enables us to see the sequence of activities that make up the project critical path. This is the chain of linked events that leads to the shortest project completion time. It's also a sequence of events in which delay will lead to the delay of the whole project rather than just a delay of a single activity. Seeing this helps you to manage the project. You can, for example, decide to divert resources into a critical path activity and, by so doing, further reduce the project completion time. It also tells you which of the project's activities you need to focus your attention on if you are to complete the project on time.

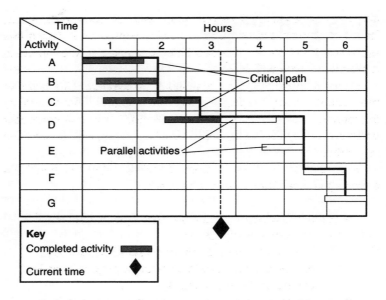

Figure 3.3: Gantt chart

All of this not only helps you to manage your project – it also helps you to do that efficiently and effectively. The Gantt chart requires limited training for its creation and use. For small projects it can even be drawn by hand on standard graph paper or paper with preprinted columns. There are also proprietary versions of wall-mounted charts with magnetic or click-in strips that can be used to create Gantt charts for projects with up to 100 activities. For larger projects – with large numbers of activities – the substantial size of the Gantt chart does cause problems. Computer display screens are often too small to provide the required level of detail and projectors suffer from low definition images. One solution to this dilemma is to use a computer to do the number-crunching and dependencies and then print out and display the day-by-day operations by using cut-and-paste sheets of paper stuck on a wall or wall board. This can act as a focus for all project discussions and can even be used as a record board with all comments, ideas, issues, problems, phone calls, etc. being written on it. Doing this bypasses the often arduous and time-consuming task of updating a proprietary type wall chart.

However, none of these suggestions will overcome the fact that the Gantt chart cannot easily or clearly show activity interdependencies. These, as you saw earlier in this chapter, occur when an activity cannot be started until a prior activity or activities are complete.

Nevertheless, the Gantt chart is popular and its significant advantages mean that it often gets used:

- **on small projects** – as a planning system that:
    - has low training demands
    - provides a direct, easily understood visual image
    - can be quickly used to generate a project 'overview'
    - can be generated manually.
- **on larger projects** – as a planning system that, in its computer-generated form, can be used, in parallel with a network system, as an aid to communication.

Networks

Network planning systems first became popular in the late 1960s and early applications included the development of the Polaris missile system and the construction of large chemical plants. Since then their use in project planning has become widespread and, not surprisingly, a variety of network types have developed. Many of these are designed to help the project plan cope with high levels of uncertainty or complexity. Examples include GERT (Graphical Evaluation and Review Technique), PERT (Programme Evaluation and Review Technique) and VERT (Venture Evaluation and Review Technique).

In this chapter you'll take a look at two of the simpler versions of network plans. Both of these use structured networks to describe the sequence of events or activities that go to make up the project. In these networks they:

- arrange these activities so that they flow from left to right
- use arrows to make up a network
- locate either squares or circles where these arrows intersect
- store information in these squares or circles called nodes.

However, these networks use these arrows and nodes in very different ways:

- **activity on arrow or AOA networks** – in these the arrow is used to represent an activity and circles are sited at either end of the arrow or activity as shown in Figure 3.4.

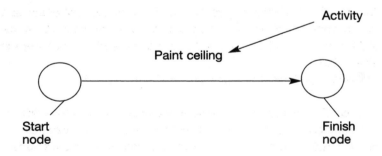

Figure 3.4: Activity on Arrow example

- **activity on node or AON networks** – in these the activity is represented by a square or box and arrows are used to link the activities as shown in Figure 3.5.

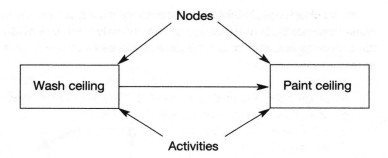

Figure 3.5: Activity on Node example

Each of these types of network has its own set of advantages and disadvantages as you'll now see.

Activity on Arrow networks

You've already seen in Figure 3.4 that the basic element of this sort of network is an arrow. When this is used to generate a full AOA network what you get is the sort of network that's shown in Figure 3.6.

When you look at this network what you see is that:

● The finish node or event of one activity is also the start node or event of the following activity – as we can see with activity C whose finish node (no. 3) is the start node for both the Dummy activity and Activity E.

● Activities can take place at the same time – as with activity B and activity C, for example.

● Several activities can emerge from a single event or node (activities B and C from node 2) or merge into one event or node (activities D and E into node 5).

- Interdependent activities can be shown by connecting their start/finish nodes with a Dummy activity (shown as a dotted line) that has no I.D. and zero duration.

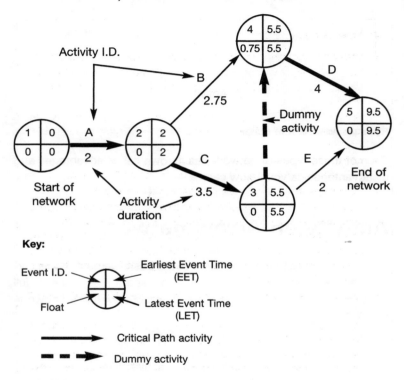

Figure 3.6: Full AOA network

- Earliest Event Time (EET) and Latest Event Time (LET) can be calculated by following the process given in Figure 3.7.
- The difference between the time available and the time required for an activity is call the Float or Slack of that activity – as in Activity B which has a float or slack of 0.75

hours and a duration of 2.75 hours, starts at 2 hours from network start, but need not finish until 5.5 hours after network start.

EET and LET calculation

- Starting at the first event write the figure '0' in the EET location.
- Move to event 2 and add the duration of activity A to the EET for event 1 – giving an EET of 2 – and write this in the EET location for event 2.
- Follow through the network adding each activity duration to the previous event's EET and writing the result into the next EET location.
- Where activities merge you'll get two figures for the finish event's EET. Write only the highest figure into the next EET location.
- Remember that dummy activities have a zero duration.
- Continue to the last event (No. 5 in this network) and write the figure generated for the EET into both the EET and the LET space.
- Starting from the last event, move backwards through the network subtracting the duration of the activity that you're following from the LET at its finish event and then writing that figure into the LET space at its start event.
- Where two activities emerge, write the lowest LET into the event space.
- Continue until you reach the first event where you should have a figure for its LET which is the same as the figure for its EET. If you haven't, then you've made a mistake – probably where two or more activities merge. Go back and retrace your EET path checking the figures as you go. If these are correct, retrace your LET pathway until you find the mistake.

Figure 3.7: EET and LET calculation

Network float or slack can be used to smooth project resource usage by starting later – or to reduce the cost of completing the activity by using less resource.

Generating and using an AOA network requires training and experience. But, despite having a visual impact that is lower than a Gantt chart, the AOA network does bring benefits. These include the ability to quickly and easily work out the implications of activity duration changes since the network does not need to be redrawn. It also enables the project manager to examine the limited trade-offs that might be available between Outcome, Cost and Time (see Crashing later in this chapter). AOA networks are usually, but not always, computer generated and have been used to considerable effect on large and complex projects.

Activity on Node networks

In Figure 3.5 you saw that the basic element of an AON network looked like this:

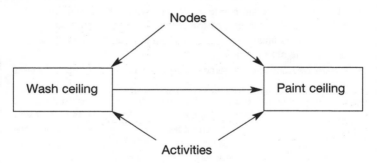

When this is used to generate a full AON network what you get is the sort of network that's shown in Figure 3.8.

The information carried in each of these nodes is generated in the same way as that for the AOA network except the backward pass generates latest start times rather than latest event times.

The AON network has no equivalent to the dummy activity of the AOA network and activity D is shown as being dependent upon activities C and B. The advantages of the AON network include:

- its ability to cope with change – since information rather than the network has to be changed
- its ability to provide the project manager with trade-off related information (see Crashing later in this chapter)
- the speed – relative to AOA networks – of its computer-driven versions.

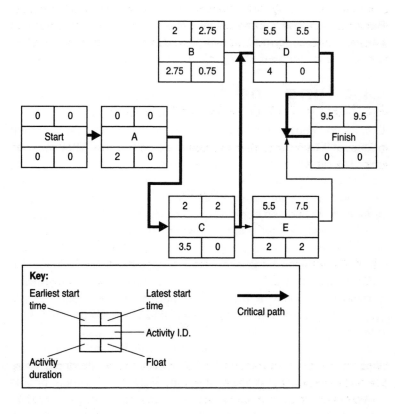

Figure 3.8: Full AON network

Its disadvantages include:

- complex calculations involved
- network diagrams are not easy to understand or follow
- considerable training and experience needed for effective use.

Because of these factors, AON networks tend to be used in a computer-driven form and on large and complex projects.

Crashing and fast-tracking

Life, as you know, doesn't always work out the way that you want or expect it to. Your projects are no exception to this. They exist, as you saw in Chapter 1, in an environment that is increasingly competitive and volatile. As a result, you're going to be confronted, at some time in your career as a project manager, with the need to reduce the scheduled duration of a project to meet a new deadline. This can happen, for example, when the project is part of the development of a new product; a product whose time-to-market has to be reduced because of oncoming competitive products, or when significant incentive payments are introduced because early completion becomes a 'must-have' situation for the client.

Project 'crashing' is a way of achieving this reduction in project duration. In its simplest form, it reduces the project duration by reducing the time of one or more of the critical path activities to a 'less-than-normal' duration. This is achieved by assigning more labour to project activities – in the form of overtime or more people – or by assigning more resources, such as more material or bigger, better, faster equipment. However, all of these will result in an increase in the project cost. But crashing isn't a 'never-mind-the-cost' approach. In it's fullest and best form it's based on an analysis of the trade-off between time and cost; a trade-off that reduces the project duration while minimising the cost of crashing.

Achieving this takes time and effort. The project team has to estimate the crash time and crash cost for each activity and then generate an estimate for the total crash time, total crash cost and the crash cost per week. The outcome is often a graph like the one in Figure 3.9:

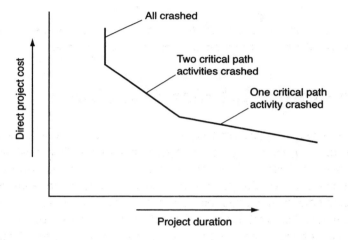

Figure 3.9: Project crashing

'Fast-tracking' is an alternative to crashing. Using it involves taking activities that would normally be done in series and then doing them partly in parallel. The word 'partly' is key here. You would not, for example, normally start constructing a project outcome until the design was completed. However, when fast-tracking, you can start constructing parts of the outcome in areas where you felt confident that the design was complete and stable – without waiting for the entire design to be completed. Obviously the activities that you fast-track should not be interdependent. Fast-tracking involves risks. Use it and you run the risk of needing to rework some of your earlier activities with the consequent increase in costs. But, when fast-tracking is used with care, this usually doesn't happen.

Resources

A resource is a part of the stuff that gets a project 'on the road'. It is anything that's needed to do the work necessary to complete an activity. This throws the net in a pretty wide arc – money, tools, equipment, people, information, skills, knowledge, materials – they're all resources. Planning these resources and making sure that they are there when you need them is a key factor in project success. But in real life, this doesn't always happen. The resources that you need aren't always there when you need them or in the quantities that you need. As a result, achieving the plans that you had for your project begins to look remote. When this sort of thing happens you need to do something about it if you are going to get your project back on course. So let's look at what you can do to make sure that the resources needed are there:

- when you need them
- in the required amount.

Activity slack

You saw earlier in this chapter that you can exploit the presence of float or slack in your project network in a number of ways. This can be done, for example, by:

- starting the activity later but completing it on time – thus shifting the time frame of the resource usage
- starting the activity as soon as possible and completing it on time – thus reducing the rate of resources usage
- splitting the total period of resource usage into several separate periods with a cumulative total duration equal to the original duration – thus shifting the time frame of resource usage.

All or any of these will help you to level or smooth the pattern of resource usage for the project as a whole – resulting in fewer or smaller peaks and troughs in that pattern. Doing this on small projects is a simple enough process and can be done by hand. On larger projects – with more activities and a wider range of resources – the process of resource leveling becomes increasingly complicated. As a result, computer systems are used on these projects.

Heuristics

In the world of projects, resource heuristics are commonsense rules (or sets of rules) intended to increase the probability of solving a resourcing problem. These are rules that:

- are based on previous experience
- have proved to produce results that are good but not 'the best'
- are easy to apply and understand.

Examples of these heuristics are:

- do critical path activities first
- do activities with the most subsequent critical path activities first
- do activities with the most subsequent activities or highest resource demands first
- do shortest activities or those with smallest float first.

These and other 'rules of thumb' represent simple and realistic solutions to resourcing problems; solutions that can be quickly and cheaply applied.

Computers and project planning

These days there are few of us who don't own or have access to a desktop or laptop computer. Some of these are high powered, using the latest technology, and some are slow but steady. But, whatever their speed or antiquity, they all bring with them the potential to relieve you of much of the number crunching that goes with project planning. Doing this, of course, needs the 'right' sort of software. But when it comes to project software packages, multiplicity seems to be the key word. A recent survey of websites selling project management (PM) software listed some 358 separate sites, each extolling the virtues of their unique software package. A survey of PM software packages in common and general use identified some 38 different packages while a survey of commonly used project, program and related software conducted by a popular project management magazine listed some 48 packages. What all of this tells us is that any attempt to survey all of these and guide you towards what might be a 'best buy' for project planning would not only be unrealistic and foolish, it would also generate another book at least as big as this, and one that would be out of date before it was published!

However, what this book will do is to identify some of the factors that you need to be clear about before you embark on your adventure with computer planning. Thinking through and being clear about these factors is an important step and one that's often overlooked or given scant attention in the helter-skelter rush to buy the newest software.

First, you need to understand that, while many of these packages are called *project management* software, that is what they don't do. Managing your project is your job – not the computer's. What the best of these packages will help you to do is to schedule or plan your project, not manage it.

Second, you need to think about your projects – about their nature, size and complexity. Try, for example, to decide if they involve more than 500 activities or use multiple resources or if there is a high level of uncertainty about activity durations. Ask yourself about how many people outside the project team you'll need to keep informed about project progress and at what level of detail. Try to decide if you'll need to update the project plan frequently or to use resource smoothing or allocation. When you've got the answers to these questions then you're ready to move on to thinking about the sort of software that you need.

Third, you need to be clear about your needs. You've already seen that there are a huge number of so-called project management software packages on the market. Most, but not all, are designed to help you to plan your project. But the ways in which they do it are different and it's these differences that will lead you to buy one package or to reject another. The ease with which you can enter, model and schedule your project will be, for some of you, the critical factor in your choice. For others, it will be whether the package can handle costs or resources or a particular sort of report. What you have to do is to identify the characteristics of the package that you want. Do you, for example, want it to be capable of generating AOA networks and Gantt charts or AON and Precedence diagram networks? Try to work out how many activities and nodes you want it to be able to handle and decide what sort of limitations you will accept in the way that these are identified. The range of calendar time that's built into the software is important as is its ability to smooth or allocate resources and handle costs and sub-projects. High levels of user friendliness are vital – but you don't want to get lost in a maze of menus. The software's outputs and reports must tell you and your clients what you both want to know. You'll need an understandable but comprehensive manual and software support – as and when you need it.

Fourth, and finally, you must make sure that the software you choose is compatible with your computer – its speed, hard disk capacity, RAM size and operating system version can be important.

It's worth looking at several programs and trialling these so that you get a good feel for what they can and can't do. While your 'shopping list' of these software packages will probably include such popular, versatile and well-proven packages as Artemis, MS Project, Merlin, Cresta and Open Plan, it's important that you find one that:

- you are comfortable with
- produces the sort of results that you want.

Use the checklist below when you are assessing these packages.

Project Planning Computer Software Checklist

Use this feature list in your assessment of project planning software.

Network/Chart:	• Gantt chart
	• AOA
	• AON
	• All or most of above
Calendar:	• Range of years
	• Number of working days/week
	• Nonworking days (statutory holidays etc.)
Events/Activities	• Maximum number
	• Identification restraints (alpha-numeric, number of characters)
Access, ease of use and support	• Menus
	• Help screens/website
	• Data entry
	• User manual
	• User hotline
	• Training
	• User group/blog

Reports	• Standard report range
	• User defined reports
	• Graphics
Resources	• Resource allocation
	• Resource range
	• Resource type
Operating system	• Current
	• Known updates due
	• Future proof
	• Firewall/Virus proofing
Hardware	• Needs new?
	• Current OK?

It's also just as important that you put some time and effort into getting to know your chosen program's idiosyncrasies and quirks – before you use it for real.

Chapter checklist

Well done! Again you've covered a lot of ground in this chapter. Use the list below to check out where you've got to. If you've missed something or didn't understand it go back to the page given and read it through again.

● A project plan enables us to convert project objectives into concrete realities (page 48).
● The first step in creating a project plan is to list the activities needed, the completion and start times of these activities and the resources needed (page 50).
● The detail level of the above must be relevant to your plan (page 52).

- Some activities are interdependent (page 53).
- Plans can be:
  - Gantt charts (page 55)
  - Activity on Arrow (AOA) networks (page 59)
  - Activity on Node (AON) networks (page 63).
- Each of these has its own set of advantages and disadvantages (pages 57, 62, 63).
- Project durations can be shortened by using Crashing and Fast-Tracking (page 64).
- Resource usage can be smoothed or levelled by using Activity Slack and/or Heuristics (page 66).

INSTANT TIP

Detailed, systematic, team-involving planning is the single most important thing that project managers do.

04

Who's in charge?

Your project will need to be managed and the way in which you do that will have a considerable influence upon whether it rises into success or falls to failure. In this chapter you'll take a look at the role of the project manager, the differences between day-by-day managing and managing a project, and the skills and abilities that a project manager needs. By the end of the chapter you'll be a lot clearer about the skills that you need to be an effective project manager, including the ability to communicate, lead, motivate, make decisions and negotiate.

Projects and project managers

A project, as you saw in Chapter 1, is a discrete 'parcel' of interconnected activities that are all dedicated towards the goal of achieving a unique outcome at a particular cost and by a particular time. But these activities don't and won't happen spontaneously – they need the catalyst of people to achieve that end point. But people need to be managed, informed, persuaded and motivated. Nor will the materials, information and equipment needs of your project be answered accidentally; the appearance (and departure) of the answers to these needs will have to be carefully arranged, planned and scheduled. But that's not all that's needed. For your project itself will also need to be defended, sold or championed against the fluctuating tides and intrigues of the 'politics' that abound both within and without your organisation. As the manager of your project, all of these and many more activities are your responsibility.

But, you might say, these – apart from the references to a project – are very much the same as the sort of activities that you undertake as a day-by-day manager.

Day-by-day managers and project managers

Both of these roles – the day-by-day manager and the project manager – are present in almost all organisations. But they are very different – both in what they do and how they do it. For day-by-day managers are concerned with continuity and consistency on an on-going timescale. Their 'rolling responsibilities' continue as long as they are employed in a management role. When they leave that management role, someone else will be appointed or step in to take over those responsibilities. The primary purpose of all day-by-day management roles is the achievement and continuing support of the long-term survival of the organisation. As you saw in Chapter 2, this long-term survival is the primary concern of all organisations. They achieve this by being good at generating replicas or variants of their core products or services; they are about stability, continuity and repetition. The day-by-day managers who work for and in these organisations are often, but not always, functional specialists. They are, for example, engineers, accountants, sales managers, marketers, social workers or bankers.

Project managers are different. They do not act as functional specialists; they are generalists, facilitators and enablers. Their responsibilities are transient; lasting only as long as the project and focusing on the creation of the project's unique outcome within the constraints of a defined timescale and a limited budget. Once the project's outcome is complete, the role of the project manager and its associated responsibilities are over and done with.

But, for you, as a day-by-day manager, the jump to becoming a project manager will not be a 'leap into the dark'. For, despite their significant differences, the roles of the day-by-day manager and the project manager still have much in common. As managers, they both need to be able to:

- lead
- communicate
- motivate
- negotiate
- make decisions.

So, let's look at how you, as a project manager, will use and apply these skills in your project; skills that you have probably already learnt and developed as a day-by-day manager or supervisor.

Leading and the project manager

Over the ages, leadership has emerged in many styles, shapes and forms. Some of these resulted in dramatic, nation-shifting events, such as wars, while others led to new religions or philosophies, such as Buddhism. Our history is rich in legends that tell us about these events and the men and women who caused them.

But in the work-a-day world of the twenty-first century things are different.

For leadership, which at its core is about influencing others, has become accessible to us all. If you doubt this, then check whether you've ever:

- convinced somebody working for you to do something different
- influenced another manager to think or act differently
- sold a new idea to your boss
- got your department or section to change the way it did things in a significant process.

You might even have influenced your whole organisation to change direction!

In all of these situations you've exerted influence. Doing that and producing change – whether large or small – means, quite simply, that you've demonstrated leadership. The detail of the when, how, what and why of your leading – however brief and limited it might have been – will have depended upon your personality, the work situation, and the problem at hand.

But, you might say, isn't doing those things part of the day-by-day manager's job?

The answer is that, for most of the time, it isn't. For, as a day-by-day manager, most of your time is spent forecasting, planning, organising, co-ordinating and controlling. Being a leader is about something else. It involves exerting a directing influence; an influence that's focused on tomorrow and the day after. As someone once put it, 'Managers think about today. Leaders think about tomorrow.' In the larger world outside our organisations our leaders paint their leadership on much broader canvases using 'colours' that can be spiritual, political or international.

However, if you think about what goes on inside your organisation you will soon realise that being a manager and being a leader aren't mutually exclusive – you can manage and you can also lead. But being one doesn't automatically mean that you are or can be the other. For being good at leading doesn't necessarily mean that you are good at managing, or vice versa. Perhaps the right way, for most of us, is a combination of the two – the ability to influence backed up by the ability to plan, organise, co-ordinate and control.

So, given that you already know how to manage, how can you become more of a leader and what's the 'right' way to do that leading?

Unfortunately the textbooks of management are full of views, opinions and theories about leadership and leading. While the good thing about all this is that it gets us away from the 'leaders are born' school of thought, the bad thing is that it's often confusing. However, there does seem to be a sort of consensus that the 'right' style of leadership depends upon a number of things. Amongst the more significant of these you'll find:

- the situation in which the leading is being done
- the culture of the organisation
- what the task is or what's being done
- how the followers like to be led.

Complicated, isn't it? When you think about all of this complexity, you'll soon come to an important conclusion – that there can't be a single unique style of leadership that will always produce the best results in all circumstances.

When you think about this it soon begins to make sense. For example, the style of leadership that works in a battlefield situation will be very different from the style that works in a 'work-a-day' routine office situation. Similarly, the leadership style that gets results when a team is doing a routine task will be different from the style that's needed when the team task demands high levels of creativity. What this means is that getting results with your project leadership is a demanding situation. For not only are you going to have to take into account the needs of both the task in hand and the people working with you on that task – you're also going to have to find a way to answer both of them.

It also means that, because your projects are, and always will be, unique one-off events, there isn't a single 'right' style of project leadership that works for all projects. Instead, there will be a range of leadership styles, some of which will work with certain projects and project teams but will not work with other projects or project teams.

But, if you're going to be effective as a project manager then you're going to have to lead more than you manage. Your leading will need to take into account factors such as the nature of the project, the prior experience, size and make-up of the project team and the project's time, money and outcome constraints. In the end, effective project leadership is about getting the required results as and when they are needed. If you, as a project manager, are going to achieve that then you must be able and willing to communicate with all of the people who work with you or are involved in that project – and this you'll now take a look at.

Communicating and the project manager

There can be little doubt that the ability to communicate, and do it well, is an important – indeed vital – strand in the web of all our lives. In the workplace, however, there are some roles that hold effective communication at the heart of all that they do. In these roles, effective communication is a 'must-have' core skill without which little could be achieved. The project manager is, without doubt, one of those roles.

As an effective project manager you will be spending most of your time communicating with others. You'll be explaining to, informing, motivating, selling to, persuading or instructing an incredibly large group of people. This is a group that can include senior client managers, contractors, union officials, government inspectors, project team members, suppliers of goods and services and many, many others.

Doing this and doing it well starts with a fairly basic but often neglected idea – that communication is *always* a two-way process. Get hold of and absorb this idea and you'll soon find that it has a significant and positive effect upon your communications.

Here's an example: As a project manager, you're giving the project team some instructions – about what to do next and when to do it. Simple, you might think, I tell them and they hear me and then, if I'm lucky, they'll do it. But as you speak the team is giving you feedback, even though they aren't saying anything. This non-verbal feedback, often called 'body language' – is shown in a number of ways. The way they sit or stand, the expressions on their faces and whether they do, or don't, look at you – are all sending you messages. These messages will – if you know how to 'read' them – tell you:

- whether your instructions have been heard
- whether your instructions have been understood
- how they feel about what you've said.

And all without a single word being spoken!

But reading and responding to this 'body language' is only one of the communication skills that an effective project manager needs. For she or he must also be able to use both the written word – as in e-mails, letters, memos and reports – and the spoken word – as in telephone calls, voice messages and face-to-face conversations. At its core, communication is about exchanging information. As such it's an exchange that takes place in a two-way process with a rich and complex interplay of message and reply, input and feedback. Getting all of this right is incredibly important. Indeed it could be said that, without these skills, your role as a project manager is doomed to failure.

Your project communications are important; they'll enable you to exchange facts, broker information, exert influence and even, on occasions, to express emotions. They'll also be both formal and informal in nature.

When formal, your project's communications will have the aim of answering the information needs of the project stakeholders. As such they'll need to be planned with care and precision. That planning should identify who needs what, when it's needed and in what form it's needed. Issues such as the immediacy of information needs – as in e-mail or 'snail' mail – and the technology involved – as in Internet or Intranet – should be debated and resolved. These formal communications will be about project performance. As such, they should give the project stakeholders information about the:

- work that has been done since the last communication
- work that should have been done in that period
- work that is planned for the next period.
- project's budgeted and actual spend to date and the budgeted spend to completion.

These formal communications of your project can be generated in a variety of forms – such as hard copy or electronic form – and are often discussed in project progress meetings. They'll use the forms and procedures which, as you saw in Chapter 2, are about your project's change control, milestone monitoring and budget control.

The informal communications of your project are just as important as its formal communications. But they are almost always underrated or taken for granted. In fact, they happen all over the place and in innumerable casual conversations, telephone calls, chats and discussions. They are often accidental, unplanned, fortuitous and spontaneous. Despite this they will represent the majority of your communications. Using these informal communications well is crucial to the success of your project. You will not, for example, be wasting your time in the early days of your project when you visit everybody who has anything to do with the project. By doing this you lay down the framework for an informal communications network that will, in future days, support and help your management of your project.

Motivating and the project manager

The subject of what does, or doesn't, motivate people has given rise to a lot of comment and controversy. Some of the ideas generated are simple – such as 'pay them more' – and some are complex – such as the view that we become 'ego-involved' in our jobs. While our own experience tells us that the money we earn is important we also know that there are other things – such as fame, prestige and reputation – that also influence and motivate us. An American psychologist called Abraham Maslow generated one of the more accessible and interesting ideas about what motivates us. Maslow told us that 'man is a perpetually wanting animal' and identified five sets of needs that we all have:

- physiological or body needs – such as food, shelter, warmth and water
- safety needs – such as safety, security, absence of threat or risk
- love needs – such as love, affection, belongingness
- esteem needs – such as reputation, prestige and recognition
- self-actualisation needs – such as creativity and self-fulfilment.

These, he argued, act upon us in the order given above and as illustrated in Figure 4.1. That is, once you have enough food, the next or 'higher' need for safety emerges. When that need has been answered the next need – for love – emerges, is answered and so on up the pyramid of needs until we reach our need for self-actualisation. Maslow states that we do feel anxious when these first four layers of need are not met but don't feel anything when they are met. The fifth need – for self-actualisation – was described as a 'growth need' and was extended later to include additional layers for our cognitive needs (the need to acquire knowledge and then to understand that knowledge) and our aesthetic needs (the need to create and/or experience beauty, balance, structure, etc.). These needs, Maslow claimed, act differently to the lower four needs. For when they are fulfilled, they do not go away like the four lower needs; rather, they motivate us further.

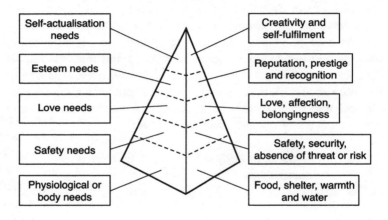

Self-actualisation needs	Creativity and self-fulfilment
Esteem needs	Reputation, prestige and recognition
Love needs	Love, affection, belongingness
Safety needs	Safety, security, absence of threat or risk
Physiological or body needs	Food, shelter, warmth and water

Figure 4.1: Maslow's Hierarchy of Needs

So, what do you, as a project manager, get out of all of this? Firstly, it tells you of something that you probably already know – that people come to work for reasons other than getting the money to answer their basic needs of food, warmth, shelter and security. They also need to have their social, creative and cognitive needs answered. When you enable or help them to do that something rather special happens – they kick out of survival mode and move up into growth mode. As a result, they become more creative, self-motivated and self-managing. They begin to do the sort of things that result in the progress of your project moving up a gear.

Secondly, it tells you that you have to give them the space to do that. This means allowing them to do things like:

- planning and controlling their own work
- taking or be involved in taking management decisions about that work.

Doing this means enlarging their project roles, giving them more responsibility and loosening the control that you exert over them. When you do this, they develop and grow. You and your project get all the benefits of this change.

Decision taking and the project manager

Sometimes decisions are big and sometimes they are small; some people take them easily and others don't take them at all. As a project manager, however, you aren't really going to have any choice about it. You will be, without doubt, a decision taker. These decisions will be about almost any aspect of the project: they'll be about people or problems or policies or plans. All of them will have to be taken within the time frame of the project and with due regard for their effect upon the key project dimensions of time, cost and outcome. You'll take these decisions in a variety of ways and places, for example:

- on your own, or
- after consulting others, or
- with the client, or
- in a project meeting.

Whoever is involved, the vital ingredient in all of these decisions is information. In a perfect world, you'll have all the good quality information you need and ample time to study it before you take your decision.

But in the real world, all managers – whether day-by-day or project – have to take these decisions with not enough information of the 'right' quality and with not enough time or money to improve or change that situation. Under these circumstances you often have to settle for a 'good enough' decision rather than one that's the best choice. One way of doing that – called a 'satisficing' process – involves deciding on and pursuing a course of action that will satisfy the minimum requirements necessary to achieve a particular goal. It doesn't attempt to identify the best solution; it merely identifies the first solution that meets the minimum requirements. Despite its limitations, satisficing does enable decisions to be taken quickly and from limited or even suspect data. When you get to Chapter 7 you'll find some other techniques that'll help you with your decision taking.

Negotiating and the project manager

We are all negotiators. We learn to do it at our mother's knee and we exploit and develop our negotiating skills at home, in the marketplace and, of course, at work. When we negotiate what we are trying to do is to resolve a situation in which what we want conflicts with what someone else wants.

There are, of course, different ways of doing this. For example, if you're negotiating with people that you don't expect to deal with again and you don't feel that you need their goodwill, then you may feel that it's right to 'play hardball'. This means going all out for a win–lose finish to the negotiation; that is you win and they lose. This often happens when houses are bought or sold, which is why house buying can be and often is such a confrontational and unpleasant experience. Similarly, if there's a great deal at stake in a negotiation, you may use legitimate 'gamesmanship' to gain advantage. If you've been involved with large sales negotiations or union-management negotiations you'll be familiar with this approach.

But neither of these ways of negotiating helps you when you want to resolve a dispute with somebody with whom you have an ongoing relationship. If you play hardball, then this creates difficulties for the other person and this will probably lead to reprisals later. Similarly, using tricks, 'games' and manipulation during a negotiation will undermine the trust that's been built up during the course of the relationship. In both of these situations and in the many other similar situations that will occur during the course of your project, being honest and open is almost always the best policy. Doing this means going for a 'win–win' outcome to your negotiation.

When you do this both you and the person you're negotiating with aim to find a solution that is acceptable to the other. When you achieve that, both of you leave the negotiation feeling that you've won, in one way or another.

As a project manager, you really don't have a choice about whether you do or don't use the 'win–win' approach in your negotiations. It's a must. Not using it will mean that you aren't trusted by those with whom you negotiate – and that won't be good for either you or your project.

But preparation is essential before any negotiation and here are a few points and questions for you to answer as you prepare for your negotiation:

- **Goals and Targets**
  Think about what you want to get out of the negotiation.
  See if you can guess what the other person wants.
- **Trades and Exchanges**
  Do you and the other person have anything that you might trade? Do you have anything that they might want?
  Would you be comfortable trading that?
- **Alternatives**
  If you don't reach an agreement with the other person:
  - does it matter?
  - what alternatives do you have?
  - does it cut you out of future opportunities?

- **Relationship issues**
  Have you and the other person got on well with each up to now? Do you want that to continue?
- **Expectations**
  What will other people be expecting from this negotiation? What has happened in past negotiations?
- **Consequences**
  What are the consequences for you and the other person of winning or losing this negotiation?
- **Compromises**
  What possible compromises might there be?

The style of your negotiating is also important. Dramatics and inappropriate displays of emotion don't work in 'win–win' negotiations. They introduce mistrust – because the other person will feel you're manipulating them – and they also undermine the rational basis of the negotiation. Nevertheless, emotions are an important part of negotiations. If what you feel about something is an important aspect of your negotiation then be open about your feelings – but do try to describe them as dispassionately as you can.

'Win–win' negotiating involves, in its simplest form, a face-to-face encounter between two individuals about some matter of shared interest. When it works, its outcome is a mutually acceptable settlement or compromise. In your project these negotiations can be about anything to do with that project. In the project's early stages issues such as the project's objectives or its organisation can be negotiated while in the later stages, plans, schedules and procedures, contracts, prices and priorities can be the subject of your negotiations.

These negotiations, as you'll see shortly, will involve a careful exploration of both your position and the other person's position. In an ideal situation, the outcome of this will be that you find that the other person wants what you are prepared to trade, and that you are prepared to give what the other person wants. But life is rarely ideal and what you'll probably both find is that there's a mismatch – you or the other person want more than the other is prepared to give. When this happens, one person must give way if an agreement is going to be reached. To balance this situation, that person will try to negotiate some form of compensation for giving way. The scale and nature of this compensation will, of course, depend upon the particular detail of the negotiation. At the end of the day, however, it's vital that both sides should feel comfortable with the final solution. Figure 4.2 illustrates some of the detail of that exploration.

When you look at this diagram you'll see that exploration goes through a sequence that involves offers, rejections and counter offers from both Buyer and Seller. This will continue until they approach agreement about a price that they can both live with – even though it's respectively higher or lower than both their expected and desired prices. But it isn't as simple or straightforward as that, for any effective negotiator will also display skills in:

- testing and summarising what has been said
- seeking information
- telling the other about how he or she feels about things
- signalling what he or she is or isn't going to do or say.

But there are also some things that a skilled negotiator will definitely **not** do:

- use words or phrases that irritate
- jump in with immediate counter proposals
- get into attack/defence sequences
- use too many arguments to support his or her case.

Doing all of this and doing it well is not an easy task. It will demand much skill, stamina and experience from you as a project manager. But it is worthwhile. For a 'win–win' negotiation is one that generates benefits beyond the negotiating table. It generates trust and sharing and having these on board in your project can only be good.

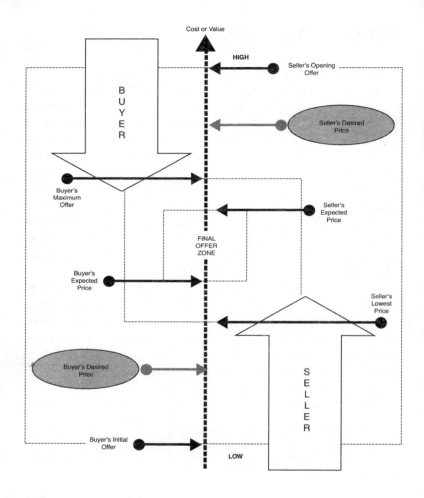

Figure 4:2: The negotiating process

Project managing

People come to project management by all sorts of routes.

You, for example, might have arrived at the role of project manager because of your background as a functional specialist. This means that you understand the project that you're working on, are able to create a good, effective project plan and efficiently manage the assignment of work to other team members. On the other hand, you might have become a project manager just because you are a good manager. As such you understand that in order to manage anything successfully you have to have and use a 'pack' of core skills. These skills – which may include some project management skills that you've picked up along the way – enable you to manage your project in ways that fit in with the way that things are managed in your organisation.

But if you're going to continue this 'evolution' and go on to become a 'real' project manager – the sort that gets results every time – then there's something else you'll need to learn. That is that you don't carry out these project management tasks and processes just because they are the 'required' or 'right' thing to do. No, you'll do them because they'll give you a much better chance for success – and success is what you want to achieve.

By now you should have begun to see the how and why of the differences between project managing and day-by-day managing. You've probably also begun to feel that it's a job that you can do – well and effectively. Use the questionnaire in Figure 4.3 to check that out.

How good a project manager are you?

Under each of the headings below ring the number which is nearest to the way that you feel that you manage your projects. Then add up your total and go to the Key section below.

1 Leadership

| I always lead my team the same way | 1 2 3 4 5 6 7 | I try to work out which way is best for this team and this project |

2 Communication

| I tell people what I think | 1 2 3 4 5 6 7 | I listen when people talk and they listen when I talk |

3 Motivation

| We pay them, isn't that enough? | 1 2 3 4 5 6 7 | I see my team as creative problem solvers |

4 Decision taking

| I let problems solve themselves | 1 2 3 4 5 6 7 | I decide quickly and with the inform-ation that I've got |

5 Negotiating

| I always want to win | 1 2 3 4 5 6 7 | Win–win is the only way |

Key

Total

5–15	You seem to be having problems!
15–25	Well done – now use your low scores to identify where you need to do better
25–35	You either walk on water – or aren't being honest!

Figure 4.3: How good a project manager you are?

Chapter checklist

Well done! Again, you've covered a lot of ground in this chapter. Use the list below to check out where you are. If you've missed something or didn't understand it go back to the page given and read it through again.

- Project managers are generalists, facilitators and enablers (page 74).
- Project managers need to be able to: lead; communicate; motivate; negotiate; make decisions (page 75).
- Leadership is about influencing others (page 76).
- The style of leadership that you use will depend upon: situation; culture; task; followers' preferences (page 77)
- Communication is a core skill for project managers (page 78).
- Communication involves body, spoken and written language (page 79).
- Communication can be formal or informal (page 79)
- People come to work for reasons other than getting the money to answer their basic needs of food, warmth, shelter and security (page 82).
- The effective project manager works with his/her team and enables them to:
  - plan and control their own work
  - take or be involved in taking management decisions about that work (page 83).
- Project management decisions are always taken with due regard for their effect upon the key project dimensions of time, cost and outcome (page 83).
- Project managers always use the 'win–win' approach in negotiations (page 85).

INSTANT TIP

Managing a project involves organising resources in ways that make sure the project is completed to defined scope, time and cost.

05

Who's in my team?

Having a good project team can make a significant difference to both the way you manage your project and its chances of success. In this chapter you'll find out about the number of people that you need in your project team, the skills and abilities that those people should have, how to choose people who will work well together in a team and how to help your team to grow and develop.

Team (*teem*), *n*: What's in a word?

The word 'team' is one that gets used a lot. It's usually used to describe the groups or squads of people who play games such as football, rugby, baseball, basketball, cricket, American football or ice hockey. But it's also used, with its cousin 'team-working', to describe some of the things that you and your co-workers do in the workplace. But all of these teams – whatever their purpose – do have something in common. They encompass the idea of several people working co-operatively together towards a common objective.

And it's this idea – about working co-operatively together – that also leads to the misuse or abuse of the word 'team'. For we all aspire to work in this way. Being a 'team-player' is seen – possibly as an echo of our tribal histories – to be a 'good' thing. Because of this we often try to kid ourselves – and others – that this co-operative working-together happens far more often than it really does. We tell ourselves and others that we work as a team – when we're probably actually working in a group that's fragmented and divisive – and we talk about our great 'team spirit' – when what we're really experiencing is a chance coincidence of our individual selfish interests.

What all of this tells you is that this word 'team' is a far-from-ordinary one. Not only is it one of the most commonly used collective nouns in the English language, it's also a word that brings with it some powerful and valuable gifts. For 'team' isn't just a word – it's also an idea, an inspiration, a way of doing things that's both aspired to and inspiring. It brings with it the idea that working together in a 'team' has the potential to enable us to achieve more than the sum of our individual achievements. As such, it's a goal for you, as a project manager, to strive for and work towards. When you reach it you and your team will have an effective way of working together; one that's both creative and productive. This will enable you, as project manager, to use your project team to focus the individual skills and abilities of your team members on the target of success for your project (see Figure 5.1).

But be warned! For a real team – unlike the many make-believe or false teams that litter our workplaces – is a rare event. It takes hard work and planning to make it happen. But when it does, you'll find that you've got:

a group of people who work together, in ways that combine their individual skills and abilities, towards a shared and meaningful outcome that they are all responsible for.

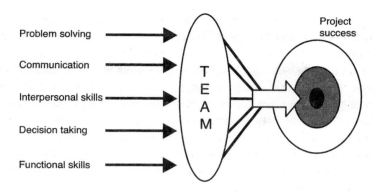

Figure 5.1: The team as a lens

A project team like this:

- makes things happen – quicker and better
- creates solutions to problems
- finds ways of moving your project up a gear.

It's also flexible, adaptable and able to:

- grow and change to meet new demands
- reinvent itself when individuals move on
- be independent of the skills and abilities and even the absence of any one member.

But to create and develop a team like this – a real team – you're going to have to work hard. You're going to have to decide things like how many people you have in your team and how they – and you – will work together. These are important decisions. Get them right and you'll create a real team – one that will significantly raise the odds on your project's success. So how does such a team come about and, just as importantly, how does it work?

Teams and people

Let's start with the obvious – teams are people events. A successful team is one that demands and flourishes on the energy and vitality of people. But a team like this isn't just any old group of people that's been thrown together. You can't, as they say, get a team – at least one that that works – by picking names at random out of your organisation's telephone directory. You have to choose these people with care. Get this choosing wrong – and end up with the wrong mix of people – and you'll have conflicts, difficulties and a poor team performance. Get it right and you'll still have conflicts and difficulties but you'll also have a good team, a team that really works.

Later in this chapter you'll take a look at the steps that you can take to make sure that you get the 'right' people in your team. But first, you need to decide how big your team is going to be.

Large or small?

When you think about this you'll soon realise that you already know quite a lot about the ways that the number of people in a team influences how well – or badly – the team works together. Your experience probably tells you, for example, that people in small groups or teams:

- have lots of face-to-face contact
- share and co-operate quite a lot, and
- directly exert influence over each other.

Similarly, you'll have seen that in large groups or teams, people have:

- less and limited face-to-face contact
- restricted sharing and co-operation, and

- indirect and general influence on each other.

These ways of behaving – and their results – will also be present in your project team. As a result, how big or small your team is will have a considerable effect upon the way that it does its work. For example, small project teams encourage co-operative working with contributions from everyone. People who work in teams like this are generally happier about what goes on in them than people who work in large teams. But when you increase the size of your project team you begin to get other benefits, benefits that result from the increasing range and diversity of skills and abilities present in that team. This means, for example, that your project problem solving will get better. The team will be able to generate more and better potential solutions for your project problems and there will be more people with the skills that you will need to implement those solutions. But that's not all that happens. For, as the size of the team increases, issues about who's in charge will raise their head and the quality of communication within the team will fall. This often means that team members who are less confident or outgoing become increasingly inhibited and potential dissenters become less willing to speak out for fear of being thought 'out of line' or uncooperative. Increasing team size also results in each individual team member having, on average, less chance of contributing to discussion. This can lead to a situation where team decisions shift away from being generated by consensus towards majority decisions that exclude minorities.

So how many people is the right size for your team? The answer to this question is, like so many things in life, a compromise. You'll need to trade-off or strike a balance between:

- the higher levels of skill and knowledge diversity and creative conflict that occur in larger teams, and
- the higher levels of participation, cohesiveness and involvement that occur in smaller teams.

But fear not, for help is at hand! The way that teams do – and don't – work has been the subject of much research and study. As a result, the range and limits of effective team size have been identified. What these tell you is that, for effective working, your team:

- shouldn't have more than ten members, and
- should – if participation and involvement are key issues – have between five and seven members.

The exact number of people that you have in your team will be influenced by factors such as:

- the size and complexity of the team task
- the skills, abilities and experience of the people available
- the time scale of the task.

If you're involved in setting your team up then you're going to have to weave all of these together into a team size and task definition that are compatible. Take on too big a task and failure will loom – unless you shift your team into being a super-team that manages and controls the activities of other smaller teams or sub teams. Take on too big a team for the task in hand and you'll finish up with a team whose members are neither stretched nor challenged – and idle hands, as they say, make mischief.

But the number of people that you have in your team isn't the only thing that influences its performance; the sorts of people that they are and the way that they do or don't work together are just as important. For if your team is going to work then it will have to provide a framework within which individual team members can find or create ways of working together and behaving co-operatively. Doing this – working well in a team – has two significant aspects:

- the roles that people carry out or take on in the team
- the ways that they behave in the team.

Let's take a look at these.

Team roles

If you look up the word 'role' in the dictionary you'll find that a role is really a set of behaviours. So, when you act out or take on a role then you behave in a certain way. You do this – adopt a role – because you think the situation that you're in demands it or because you think it's appropriate to what you're doing. You have lots of roles. You can be – and may actually be – a brother, sister, father, mother, son, daughter, boss, supervisor, manager or co-worker. All of these are roles. When you carry out one of these roles you behave in a way that's:

- relevant to the role, and
- different from the way that you behave when you carry out another role.

We all take up roles when we work in a team. Initially, these will probably be to do with a particular skill or area of experience that we have. You might, for example, be the team's accountant or software specialist – because, outside the team, you have expertise in or relevant experience of these functional roles. The nature and range of a project team's functional roles will reflect the nature of the project outcome. For example, the team on a new office block project will contain civil engineers, structural engineers, electrical engineers and heating and ventilation specialists while the team for the production of a new book will involve a text editor, a production editor, a graphic designer, a cost accountant, a printer, sales personnel and a marketing person.

But as your team gets used to working together and matures you might find yourself carrying out roles that aren't related to your functional abilities. You might, for example, find yourself:

- coming up with new ideas
- defusing conflict or tension
- looking after the team chores
- analysing what's happening
- challenging the position or attitudes of the rest of the team.

The more of these team roles that get taken up, the more productive and flexible your team will be. It may even get to the point where the team operates in ways that are independent of individual efforts or skills. One of the more accessible ways of looking at these team roles is the one that's been developed by Dr Meredith Belbin.

Belbin team roles

When Dr Belbin did his research on teams he looked at groups of managers who were playing team management games as a training exercise. Using psychometric tests, he examined the characteristics of both successful and unsuccessful teams and tried to find out if these had any common characteristics. What he found was that successful teams were made up of people who were able to make sure that some eight, quite different, team roles were carried out. Belbin's original outlines and titles for these roles are shown in Figure 5.2.

He also found that we, as individuals, all have:

- a 'primary' team role that we would prefer to carry out, and
- a 'secondary' team role that we will carry out if:
  - our primary role has been taken up by a more powerful individual, or
  - no one else in the team is able to carry out this secondary role.

Belbin Team Roles

- **Chairman** – described as being 'calm, self-confident and self-controlled', this role clarifies group objectives and sets agendas.
- **Company Worker** – a hard-working practical organiser who turns other team members' ideas into manageable tasks.
- **Shaper** – 'outgoing and dynamic', this role is the task leader, uniting ideas and shaping the application of team effort.
- **Plant** – 'individualistic and unorthodox', this role is the ideas generator for the team but can be detached from practicality.
- **Resource Investigator** – often described as the fixer of the team, this role has high communication skills and social acceptability.
- **Monitor–Evaluator** – the analyst of the team who tends to be 'sober, unemotional and prudent'.
- **Team worker** – 'mild and sensitive', this role listens and communicates well and often smooths conflict.
- **Completer–Finisher** – a perfectionist who has to check every detail.

Figure 5.2: Belbin team roles

Belbin's original team roles were later modified to include a Specialist role and to change the role title for the Chairman role to Co-ordinator and the title for the Company Worker role to Implementer. The Specialist role is described as one that views the team task or objectives through the medium of and with the limitations of their area of individual expertise.

Get people who can carry out these roles in your team and you'll have a team that:

- is balanced and effective
- makes the best use of its resources
- has the ability to bounce back from disappointments
- displays adaptability
- contains a few members who are creative
- has limited dependence on key members.

The Belbin approach to team composition management has developed self-assessment questionnaires to enable you and other potential team members to identify your primary and secondary team roles. But this isn't the only commercially available approach to team selection available. You can find out more about these on the Internet where you'll come across more information about the Belbin approach and discover other approaches, such as the Margerison–McCann approach and the Management Team Role Indicator developed by S. P. Myers.

By now you should be quite clear about how important it is to make sure you get the right mixture of complementary skills, abilities and experience in your team. If you do this then the resulting team will have a potential that exceeds, by orders of magnitude, the sum of the abilities and skills of its individual members. This will happen because your team is made up of people who:

- have been chosen for their interpersonal skills as much as their functional skills
- are able to adjust their team role and function to complement those of others in the team
- provide a balanced range of both external and internal roles.

But choosing the 'right' people is only the beginning of your team – as you'll see in the next section.

Getting together

Let's assume, for the moment, that you've decided how many people you want in your team. You've also reviewed and chosen the functional skills that you need them to have and then selected the people who have these skills together with the role and interpersonal skills that your team needs.

So, you say to yourself, what do I do next? The answer is that you call your first team meeting. Sounds obvious, doesn't it? But your first team meeting isn't just a social, 'getting-to-know-you', event. It's actually a lot more than that. It's the beginning of the process by which the motley collection of individuals that you have chosen will evolve, change and develop into an effective, working, results-generating team.

It may also be the first time that some of you meet each other. Despite, or rather because of this there should be no exemptions, no acceptable 'sorry-I've-a-diary-clash' excuses for non-attendance for this meeting. It's a mandatory, must-be-there, meeting for *all* the team members. The way that this meeting is scheduled and arranged should reflect its importance. The invitation to attend must let the team members know that attendance is a 'must-do'.

But the success of this first meeting will start before then. For before this meeting you have to decide:

- where it's going to be held
- what you're going to talk about.

Let's look at each of these in turn.

Team spaces

The best place to have the first meeting of your team is in the team space. It's important that you have a dedicated team room. Sharing a workspace with other groups of people or having a part-time team space just doesn't work. Having a dedicated team space not only gives the team privacy; it also makes a clear and unambiguous statement to the rest of the organisation, a statement that says:

- this team is here, and
- this team is important.

But that's not all that a dedicated workspace will do for your team. It also provides a physical focus for what team members are doing for the team, a place where they can pick up on their team duties where they left off, a space that's the team space. This team space should be one:

- that's convenient for all team members to access
- that all team members feel mentally and physically comfortable in
- where team members can clearly hear – without interruption – all that's said
- that has all the facilities that the team needs – such as chairs, tables, filing cabinets, flip chart boards, audio visual aids, computers, power points, etc.
- that has or is close to overnight stay facilities – if team members need them
- that's private and adequately secure so that team business can be conducted in private.

The Team Charter

The primary purpose of this first meeting is the generation, discussion and agreement of a document that identifies the why, what, when and how of the team. This is a document that will provide the answers to obvious questions such as 'What are we going to do?', 'How long will it take?' and 'Who are our customers?' But it will also answer more subtle – but just as important – questions such as 'How are we going to work together?', 'Will we all be involved in key decisions?' and 'What principles are important to us as a team?' The answers to these and other questions make up what's often called the Team Charter. They need to be hammered out in this first meeting. As project manager you should have thought through where you stand on the key issues and prepared a draft document for discussion. This should tell the team about:

- its task – what, by when, at what cost, etc.
- the project's key customers – names, roles, expectations
- the project stakeholders – names, expectations, conflicts.

It should also give them some idea of the options for:

- how communications are to be managed with customers and stakeholders and between team members
- how team performance will be measured – key results, milestones, and outcomes
- what procedures and rules will be used – must-be-done rules, areas of discretion
- how the team will work together – principles of team operations.

Remember that this will be a draft and try to get the level of detail right. Too much detail and people will feel that any real discussion has been pre-empted; too little detail and the discussions will produce nothing more than a series of 'broad-brush' generalities. It's worth starting off with a package of statements that define, irrespective of the detail level of your draft, the core principles of the way in which you want the team to operate. Good examples would be:

● Working together is more productive than working apart.
● Joint decisions are stronger than solo ones.
● Team meetings are jointly owned.

Once the meeting starts, it's important that project team members are given the space to freely express any fears or concerns that they might have. There's no point in having a project team meeting in which people can't freely speak their minds and know that they'll be listened to. If you, as project manager, do this, by the end of this first meeting you'll have a group of people who have begun to get to know each other and have either:

● signed on to the Team Charter, or
● agreed that your draft of this Team Charter needs to be revised.

In the end, the content, detail, form and structure of your Team Charter is down to you and your team. But it's important that *everybody* on the team understands and signs up to it.

Team building

You've already seen that the first team meeting is important – if not vital – to the creation of the Team Charter. But that's not all that happens there. It's also the beginning of the team building process.

This process, which takes team growth and change and builds on them, is a slow and gradual one. It takes time for the team to complete its journey from being a collection of individuals to becoming a cohesive, supportive, flexible and productive team. To do that your project team members will have to change, develop and grow. It's a journey that will take them from the inhibited watchfulness of their first meetings, through conflict and the development of their own 'home-grown' set of rules and standards to, finally, become a team. One of the more accessible views about how this happens tells us that a team 'grows' through four stages called 'forming', 'storming', 'norming' and 'performing' (Figure 5.3). This is a process that takes time and needs help and support.

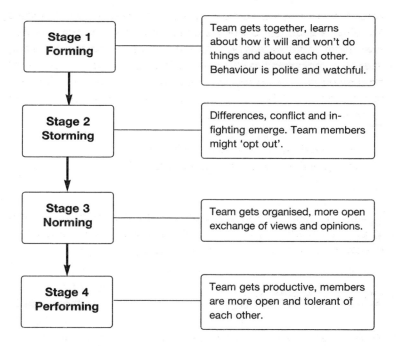

Stage 1 Forming — Team gets together, learns about how it will and won't do things and about each other. Behaviour is polite and watchful.

Stage 2 Storming — Differences, conflict and in-fighting emerge. Team members might 'opt out'.

Stage 3 Norming — Team gets organised, more open exchange of views and opinions.

Stage 4 Performing — Team gets productive, members are more open and tolerant of each other.

Figure 5.3: Steps and stages of team building

At this point, it's important to realise that the route that each team follows on this journey to becoming a team is unique to that team. It has to be, since that team itself is unique. But despite this uniqueness there are some basic common factors that are important. One of these is about spending a lot of time together, even to the point of working in the same office or suite of offices. A lot of what happens in the team-building process is informal. It's about getting to know each other, getting to know and respect each other's strengths and weaknesses, finding ways of working together. There often isn't time for this to take place outside the day-to-day operations of the project; it's a do-it-as-we-go process. It's also a process that takes place better and more quickly when people are in close proximity to each other. Walls and doors get in the way. In large teams this will mean dedicated space for the full-time staff. In small teams or teams with part-time members this means a dedicated 'team room' to which team members come to work on the team task and in which work-in-progress is left.

Team conflict

Conflict is a necessary ingredient in the process of becoming a real team. It occurs because people don't get on with each other, because people have different attitudes or sets of values and because people have different expectations. But, most of all, in real teams, it occurs because all of the team are committed to doing their best for the team. Dealing with it isn't always easy; often feelings run high and voices are raised. But dealing with it is a must. If you sit on it, ignore it, push it under the surface of day-to-day relations, then it'll just resurface elsewhere – and be the worse for it! If you're going to deal with it effectively then you may have to change the way that you think about it. You'll have to start thinking about conflict as a constructive opportunity rather than something to be endured.

There are three key factors when it comes to dealing with conflict. They are communication, communication and communication. Doing this – communicating – involves frank, open talking and real listening. Both of these are risky. But they're essential if you're going to have a real team. Taking the risk to be open in conflict can, on the downside, lead to hurt feelings, hostility, enmity, even hatred. The up side, though, is the creation of a hard-won mutual trust and interdependence that's essential to a real team.

Chapter checklist

Now you know more about teams and, in particular, project teams. Use the list below to check out where you've got to. If you've missed something or didn't understand it go back to the page given and read it through again.

- A real team will enable you, as project manager, to focus the individual skills and abilities of your team members on the target of success for your project (page 94).
- A real team is a group of people who work together, in ways that combine their individual skills and abilities, towards a shared and meaningful outcome that they are all responsible for (page 94).
- Teams are people events (page 96).
- Effective working teams:
  - shouldn't have more than ten members, and
  - should, if participation and involvement are key issues have between five and seven members (page 98).
- Team members should:
  - have relevant functional skills
  - have good interpersonal skills, and
  - be able to adjust their team role and function to complement the rest of the team (page 99).
- It's important that you have a dedicated team space (page 104).

- Generate your team charter together, involve everyone. (page 105).
- Ensure your team goes through all its development stages Forming, Storming, Norming and Performing (page 107).
- Accept the fact that conflict is necessary to the process of becoming a real team (page 108).

INSTANT TIP

Projects need teamwork to succeed. Find the right people for your team and then get out of the way so they can make the project work.

06

Will you finish in time and where did the money go?

Once it gets going, the progress of your project will need to be:

- measured and monitored
- compared to what you had planned it to be.

When you do this, as project manager, you will get the answers to such key questions as 'Will we finish in time?', 'Will we achieve what we set out to do?' or 'Will we overspend the budget?' You'll also find out what needs to be done to keep your project 'on track'. This chapter looks at the ways in which you can do all of these effectively and efficiently.

All systems are go!

At last, it's happening – your project is underway. With that opening milestone your project makes the shift into the real world and, as a result, becomes subject to the erosive drift of time. Risks you'd thought remote and unlikely now become real, and distant possibilities evolve into oncoming certainties. These show themselves in all sorts of ways. You'll find that important material deliveries are delayed, vital equipment breaks down, key personnel go sick or are re-assigned to other projects, new technology fails to deliver – it might even snow in summer! When things like this happen, the original plans and intentions that you had for your project are challenged.

There are very, very few projects on which this sort of thing doesn't happen. It's so common that coping with it – and doing that well – is one of the most significant skills that are required by an effective project manager. In this chapter you'll learn about the ways and means that you'll use, firstly, to tell you when the activities of your project are not as they ought to be and then, secondly, to correct or limit the effects of those deviations from your project plan.

In short, the ways that you'll use to monitor and control your project.

Monitoring and controlling

The *Oxford English Dictionary* tells us that when you monitor something you observe or supervise it, or keep it under review – often by measuring or testing it at regular intervals. And so it is, or will be, with your project.

In your project, the aim of this monitoring is to tell you whether your project is – or isn't working to your original plan or budget. Doing this and doing it effectively and accurately is important. For it tells you where you, and your project, are. From this information you can then predict where you and your project are likely to be in the future. But that's not all that your monitoring can do. It will also provide you with the sort of information that you can use to motivate your project team.

If this monitoring is going to be effective it'll need to give you the answers to questions such as 'Is the painting of wall A on schedule?' or 'Have we overspent on materials?' or 'What is the project's probable finish date?' But, yet again, that's not the only information that it will give you. For it will also tell you about the where and when of your project's drifts and deviations. All of this information will enable you to begin to do something about the cause of these differences – and thus control your project and bring it back 'on track'.

What do you monitor – and when?

When it comes to monitoring your project there are two things that you have to make your mind up about before you start. These are:

- what you're going to monitor, and
- when or how often you're going to monitor it.

Let's look at each of these in turn.

In an ideal world you'd be able to monitor everything – and in real time too! But in the real world, things aren't like that and what you're going to have to do is to choose a limited number of things to monitor. This choice is one that must be made with care and thought. If you monitor too many things, you'll finish up with too much data and too little time to analyse it. But if you monitor too few or too unimportant things, you'll miss the drift or movement away from your plan for a key aspect of your project – and be unable to correct it until it is too late. Getting this balance right is important. In order to do that you have to identify your project's pulse-points. These 'pulse-points' must, of course, be related to the key features of your project – Cost, Performance and Time. The closer this relationship is, the better your monitoring will be. But that's not all that you have to take into account when deciding what you're going to monitor. For if those 'pulse-points' are going to help you to manage your project then not only must they be related to those key features – Cost, Performance and Time – they must also themselves be:

- significant
- believable and
- easy to measure and understand.

Finding project 'pulse-points' like this isn't always easy – but it can be done. For example, on a project to write a book like this one you can monitor – using the word count facility of your word processing software – the number of words written. Similarly, on a project to redecorate a room you can monitor the wall area being repainted or repapered. But just measuring 'pulse-points' like these doesn't tell you the whole story. To gain access to that, you need to be able to link them back to those two core sources of project information – the project plan and the project budget. Both of these, as you'll shortly see, are key to the process of monitoring. They'll also contain the information that you need to help you to decide the other key aspect of your monitoring – when or how often you do it.

Deciding the 'right' frequency of your monitoring measurements is just as important as deciding what to monitor. Too often and you'll drown in data; not often enough and you'll miss the early drift that leads to later major deviations. Getting it right depends on things like the overall length of the project and its risk level. For example, on most long projects, measurement and reporting on a weekly frequency would be sufficient. On short projects – in which the events of a single day can be crucial – measurement and reporting on a daily or even half-daily frequency would be warranted. Similarly, high-risk projects demand, for obvious reasons, more frequent measurements than low-risk projects. Whatever you decide, remember that in this – as in other areas – regularity is important. Regular monitoring will keep you in touch with your project – and that will enable you to manage it successfully.

Monitoring and the project plan

You saw, in Chapter 3, that your project's plan is your attempt to control the future of your project. In its initial form, this plan helps you to estimate both the cost and duration of the project. But its purpose changes once your project gets underway. Once that happens, your plan becomes a road map for your project's journey, a 'this-is-what-you-do-next' guide for the actions of you and your project team. But that isn't the only use that you can put your project plan to.

You can also use that plan as a baseline against which you can monitor the progress of your project. When you do this you'll find out where the activities of your project are with respect to your original plan or schedule. Sometimes these activities will be ahead of schedule and other times they'll be behind. Occasionally, but not often, they'll be exactly on track and up to schedule. When your project's activities are ahead of or behind schedule you'll need to decide what you are going to do about that. The project plan provides you with a framework within which you can identify and evaluate the options or choices that are available to you. To achieve this your plans must be – as you saw in Chapter 3 – clear, unambiguous, easily understood and, above all, capable of change. This act of changing or modifying your project plan is – as you will see later in this chapter – one of the ways by which you can control your project. But if that change is to be effective then it must always be preceded by and based on the data generated by the process of monitoring.

This data can often be presented and contained within the project plan itself – as in the filled-in bars of the Gantt chart and the data recorded on the nodes and arrows of the AOA networks or the nodes of AON networks.

Another way of using the project plan to present monitoring information uses milestones. These, like the milestones of our highways, can be used to mark the stages of your project's journey from start to completion. They are best set at the end or beginning of an activity – for ease of identification – and are usually limited to Critical Path activities. On a Gantt chart they can be indicated graphically by an icon such as a diamond ($\Diamond$). The unfilled $\Diamond$ represents a scheduled milestone and the filled $\blacklozenge$, a completed milestone. Your project's progress towards their achievement can also be reported in the words and dates of a milestone report that contains such information as:

Milestone no.	Scheduled date	Anticipated date	Achieved date	Notes
4	25 Jan.	–	23 Jan.	Completed ahead of schedule
5	13 Dec.	15 Dec.	–	Material delivery delay anticipated

These project milestones will tell you, as do those on our highways and roads, how far you have travelled towards the completion of your project. But they are not the only tools that we can use to monitor the status of our projects.

Monitoring by limit testing

You can also monitor how your project is coming along by using Limit Testing. This involves comparing the current achieved value of a particular activity to the value that you had planned would have been achieved by this time. If there is a difference between these, then this tells you that you need to know more about what's happening. The larger the difference, the quicker you need to know about it and the more detail you require. This technique can also, with a little imagination, be applied to other critical aspects of the project such as activity rates or project spend. Its advantages include its compatibility with most project management information systems (PMIS) and the ease of its operation. The responses and actions that are triggered by a difference – between planned and achieved – need to be relevant to its size. For example, a milestone achievement rate that is 5 per cent low will initiate an investigation, whereas a 10 per cent underachievement would cause tighter control procedures to be initiated and an increase in reporting frequency. It's also worth noting that Limit Testing can also help you to manage your time – since you only become involved when the pre-set limits have been exceeded.

Pareto analysis

Pareto or ABC analysis is another technique that you can use to monitor the progress of your project. Commonly used in inventory management, ABC analysis is based on the work of Vilfredo Pareto, a nineteenth-century Italian economist. Pareto identified the empirical relationship that is often called the 80–20 rule. When used to control inventories this identifies the 20 per cent of stock that is responsible for 80 per cent of total inventory costs. These are called Class A items. You can use this rule in your project to tell you which are the 20 per cent of activities that are responsible for 80 per cent of project labour costs or the 20 per cent of materials that are responsible for 80 per cent of the project's material costs. Once these are identified then you can make sure that they are measured and monitored more frequently. You can also use this 80–20 rule to identify those activities that are involved in or associated with the project's critical path – and then readjust your monitoring and reporting accordingly. All of this means that you can monitor those key items and activities that are significant in relation to two of your project's dimensions – Cost and Time. Pareto analysis – like Limit Testing – can also help you to use your time more effectively, by focusing on Critical Path activities. Take a look at Chapter 7 to get an idea of how you can also use Pareto Analysis to identify and solve your project's problems.

Monitoring and the project budget

Budgets are, of course, about money – and money is what keeps your project rolling along. In Chapter 1 you saw that your project's cost was one of its three key dimensions and that this cost – together with the project's duration and outcome – should be:

- clearly defined at the beginning of the project
- monitored throughout its duration
- carefully managed and controlled at all times.

You also saw that the first version of your project's total cost statement was created in the Conception Stage of your project's life cycle and then polished, refined and extended in the Birth and Development Stage. The result – your project's budget – isn't just a pot of money that's earmarked for your project. It's also an itemised and detailed summary of the intended expenditure for your project – a summary that tells you not just **what** is to be spent but also **when** that spend is to take place. In the best of budgets this sequence of project expenditure or cash flow is defined from the beginning to the end of the project. If you want to know more about how project budgets are created mark this page and go to Chapter 10, where there's more about the process of estimating and its contribution to the creation of the project budget. Don't forget to come back though – because you haven't yet finished with finding out how to monitor your project's cash flow.

Monitoring your project's cash flow is an absolute must. If you fail to do that then you put at risk your ability to achieve the targets that have been set for your project; targets that are defined in terms of Cost, Time and Outcome. But before you look at the ways in which you can do that you need to remind yourself about some of the basics about cost.

Costs

A cost, according to the *Oxford English Dictionary,* is 'that which must be given or surrendered in order to acquire, produce, accomplish, or maintain something; the price paid for a thing'. In your project, a cost will spring into being when you spend money or make a commitment to do that at some point in the future. This, for example, happens, or will happen, when you buy or order your project materials – such as bricks, steel, plastic or wood – or when you pay people for work that they have done on your project or when you hire or buy equipment to use on that project. According to the conventions of bookkeeping and accounting these are called material costs, labour costs and equipment costs respectively. But costs can also be direct – as when you charge them directly to a specific project activity – or indirect – as when you allow them to be absorbed in the overall costs of the project. These indirect costs are also often called overheads.

But those aren't the only adjectives that are attached to your project costs. For your project costs can also be said to be fixed costs – which remain at the same level irrespective of the project's degree of completion – or variable costs – which vary with (amongst other things) the rate of activity or project workload. The costs of your project will also include standard costs. These are predetermined costs that are used, initially, when estimating the cost of a project activity and then later, to monitor the cost performance of the project. These standard costs are usually generated from historic data and can be calculated for any activity or resource in the project. For example, if your project includes the activity of building a brick wall then you'll have used a standard cost for laying bricks and a standard cost for the bricks themselves. Both will be in currency units – as in Rand, yen, £ or $ – per 1,000 bricks.

When all of these – and other costs – are added together you'll have the project's total cost estimate. This, as you know, is one of the key dimensions of your project. In the early stages of your project's life it can exert a considerable influence upon whether that project is or isn't chosen – as you'll see in Chapter 10. Now, however, you need to take a look at the role that it and its component costs play in the monitoring of your project.

Project costs and monitoring

You have already seen that Limit Testing and ABC Analysis can help you with your monitoring of your project's costs. Another of the ways by which you can do this is by using what's often called the S curve (Figure 6.1). This shows you the shapes of the project's budgeted and actual cumulative spends when plotted against time. It also shows you the differences between these cumulative spends. It gets its name – S curve – from the fact that the graph for the budgeted cumulative cost usually follows an S shape. When you plot your actual cumulative project spend on the same graph you can see whether you are spending more than was budgeted for or less than that.

But what the S curve doesn't show you are the causes of the differences between the planned and actual spend. These are important, as you'll soon see.

When you look at the S curve shown in Figure 6.1 you'll see that, currently, the cumulative actual cost of your project is less than you had planned – an apparently comfortable situation, you might think.

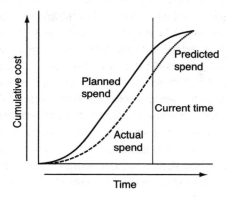

Figure 6.1: The S curve

But this could have come about for a number of reasons. It could have happened, for example, because:

- the work completed was on schedule or even ahead of schedule but was costing less than you had planned, or
- the work completed was behind schedule but was costing more than had been planned.

The differences between these two are significant. One of them – the lower than budgeted achieved cost – means that your future costs are likely to be less than the budgeted level while the other – the higher than budgeted achieved cost – means that your future costs look likely to exceed the budget.

But which one is it?

Earned value

Earned Value Analysis (EVA) is probably the best way of answering this question – and telling you what is actually happening. Most effective when you apply it to a single element or part of your project's Work Breakdown Schedule or WBS (see Chapter 3), it provides a snapshot of what's happening. EVA uses three basic measures that are based on the actual costs incurred and cost estimates for your project. These are:

- **Projected** or **Planned Value (PV)** This cost, which is also called the **Budgeted Cost of Work Scheduled** (BCWS), is the answer to the question: 'How much did you expect to pay for the work scheduled to be done by now?'
- **Earned Value (EV)** This cost, which is also called the **Budgeted Cost of Work Performed** (BCWP), is the answer to the question: 'How much did you expect to pay for the work that was actually done by now?'
- **Actual Cost (AC)** This cost, which is also called the **Actual Cost of Work Performed** (ACWP), is about the answer to the question: 'What was the actual cost of the work completed by now?'

These are then used to calculate a set of variances. A variance, by the way, is a difference between what is expected to happen and what actually happens. These are:

- **Schedule Variance (SV)** This gives us the answer to the question: 'Are you ahead of or behind schedule?' and is calculated as follows:

    SV = EV – PV or
    SV = BCWP – BCWS

A negative value for SV means that you are behind schedule.

- **Cost Variance (CV)** This gives us the answer to the question: 'Are you spending more or less than budget?' and is calculated as follows:

CV = EV – AC or
CV = BCWP – ACWP

A negative value means that you are over budget.

You can see all of these in Figure 6.2.

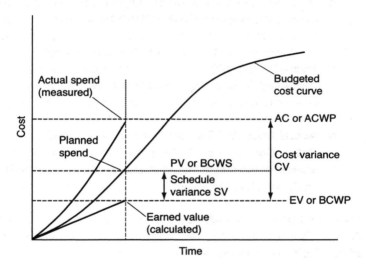

Figure 6.2: EVA chart

You can also use these measures (Projected or Planned Value (PV), Earned Value (EV) and Actual Cost (AC)) to give you an indication of how far you are ahead of or behind schedule and how far you are over or under budget. These are generated by calculating the **Schedule Performance Index (SPI)** and the **Cost Performance Index (CPI)** as follows:

SPI = EV/PV (Note: < 1 means behind schedule)
CPI = EV/AC (Note: < 1 means over budget)

These indices can be used to forecast:

- **Estimate at Completion (EAC)** This attempts to give the answer to the question: 'At the rate achieved to date how much will this activity cost at completion?' and is calculated as follows:

EAC = Budgeted Cost at Completion/CPI

- **Variance at Completion (VAC)** This attempts to give you the answer to the question: 'At the rate achieved how much will you be over or under budget at completion?' and is calculated as follows:

VAC = Budgeted Cost at Completion – EAC

- **Schedule at Completion (SAC)** This attempts to give you the answer to the question: 'At the given rate how long will the work take to be completed?' and is calculated as follows:

SAC = Forecast Duration/SPI

Earned Value Analysis (EVA) is a widely accepted industry best practice for project management. It's now enshrined the American National Standards Institute/Electronic Industries Alliance Standard on Earned Value Management System guidelines that was revised in 2002 and given a new identification number – ANSI/EIA-748-A-1998 (R2002). Used by many government departments and commercial organisations, EVA measures your project's progress against the baseline of your project budget and plan. Figure 6.3 contains an example of its use in which earlier or more frequent monitoring might have saved the day!

EVA example

Part of your project requires a brick wall to be built on prepared foundations. The wall, when complete, will require 4000 bricks, to be put in place over a planned period of 20 days and at a total budgeted cost of £500. After 10 days your monitoring tells you that £300 has been spent and 1500 bricks erected.

PV or BCWS = planned bricks × budgeted cost
                 = (4000 × 10/20) × 500/4000
                 = £250

EV or BCWP = actual bricks × budgeted cost
                 = 1500 × 500/4000
                 = £187.5

AC or ACWP = actual cost to date = £300
SV = EV − PV = £ (187.5 − 250) = − £62.5
CV = EV − AC = £ (187.5 − 300) = − £112.5
SPI = EV/PV = 187.5 /250 = 0.75
CPI = EV/AC = 187.5/ 300 = 0.625

These tell you that you are over budget and behind schedule. They will also tell you that, unless you do something about this situation, this activity will finish with a total cost of £800 (£300 over budget!) and an achieved duration of 26.6 days (almost 7 days over plan!).

Figure 6.3 EVA example

Risk monitoring

Projects, as you saw in Chapter 1, are always risky ventures. When you get to Chapter 9 you'll see how important it is to assess and do something about those risks. There you'll see that, before that project is sanctioned, you'll need to:

- identify the source and nature of each foreseeable risk
- reduce those risks or, if possible, eliminate them
- decide whether or not you will accept the risks that remain.

Doing all of this helps you to realistically estimate the needs of your project and bring it through the project selection process.

But your projects can never be risk free and as a result you need to monitor and assess these risks throughout the whole of the project's life. Doing this and doing it well is just as important as monitoring your project costs and plan. Done well, it will make your risks more visible. But the list of risks that you identified earlier in your project's life cycle will change as the project matures. New risks will develop or anticipated risks may disappear. Your risk monitoring should enable you to cope with these changes and:

- track previously identified risks
- spot and analyse any new risks that have appeared.

Controlling

Controlling is an implicit part of managing. It's applied to all sorts of things – people, costs, schedules, deliveries and completions. When you control something your aim or objective is to make sure that the future that you want actually happens. But that's not all that controlling is or does. Controlling is:

- a continuous process
- forward looking
- very closely linked with planning.

It's also a very important part of managing a project.

When you find that the activities of your project are not as you'd planned, then you need to do something about it. The actions that you take must be focused on a single exclusive objective – that of bringing your project back in line with its plan or budget. That is, these actions – by which you control your project – must act to reduce the difference between what is actually happening and your project plan or budget.

But what do you do when your project is drifting 'off course'? When you dip into the annals of control theory you'll soon see that there are two ways of exerting the control that you need. These are:

- **feed-back control** – which monitors the output from some activity or process and adjusts the input to that process or activity as necessary to achieve a desired value for that output. This happens in your car when you monitor its speed and then adjust the accelerator pedal position to achieve the speed that you want (see Figure 6.4).

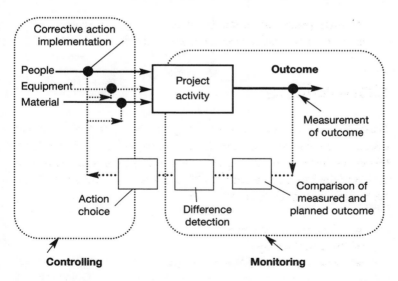

Figure 6.4: Feed-back control

● **feed-forward control** – best used where what's happening in the process or activity is well understood, feed-forward control comes into play in your car when you see a hill coming up and adjust the accelerator pedal position in anticipation of the speed reduction that the hill could cause. The car does not have to slow down at all for you to do this (see Figure 6.5).

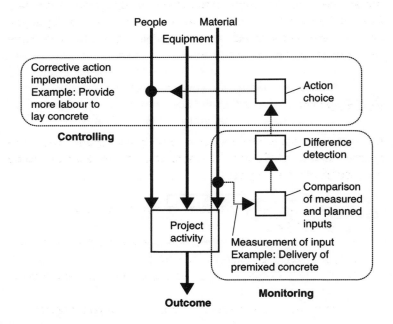

Figure 6.5: Feed-forward control

You've already seen, in Chapter 3, that you can use your project plan to help you choose what these actions are to be. Doing this will help you to identify the probable results of your 'what if we ...' proposals and test the feasibility of your alternatives. You've also seen, in the same chapter, how you can use Crashing and Fast

Tracking to reduce the scheduled completion time of a project to meet a new deadline. In Chapter 7 you'll look at some of the ways that you can use to identify effective solutions to the problems that can cause a project to drift 'off-course'. But, whatever you decide to do to exert that control and however you arrive at that decision, your control of your project must have its roots in your monitoring. For it's this monitoring that tells you when the activities of your project aren't as they ought to be. Then, and only then – when you have that information – are you able to decide what actions you need to take and then act to correct or limit the effects of those variations from your project plan.

Actions

But these actions, if they are going to bring your project back 'on-course' need to have certain characteristics. If they are going to be successful they need to be:

- appropriate – to the project, its outcome and its stakeholders
- in proportion to the size of the monitored departure from your plan or budget – or its cause.
- prompt and quick acting – to ensure that variation doesn't get out of control
- cost effective – to ensure that the cost of your control doesn't exceed its value, and
- capable of results that oppose the forces that are driving your project 'off-course' – and their causes.

Getting all of this right can take real skill and judgement. Before the event there will never be enough information for you to be *absolutely* sure that what you intend to do will work.

But not all of these variations and deviations will be small and capable of correction by the day-by-day remedial actions of your project control. They might also be substantial or significant. Variations and deviations like these can happen, for example, when new technology becomes available early in the project's life span or when detailed design work shows you that there's a better way to do something. Others will have their roots in your mistakes and errors. But, whatever their origin, nature or size, these substantial or significant changes bring with them the potential to drive your project off-course. As a result your project could fail to achieve its planned duration, cost or outcome. It is essential that you use your project change control procedure to control these potential amendments to your project. An effective change procedure is an important tool in the way that you control your project. It will, as you saw in Chapter 2, enable you to evaluate, approve or reject any proposed changes at the earliest possible opportunity.

Above all, the actions that you, as a project manager, take to control your project must be:

- based on facts – rather than opinions
- targeted solely toward keeping your project in line with it's planned, duration, cost and outcome.

Chapter checklist

Use the list below to check out where you've got to. If you've missed something or didn't understand it go back to the page given and read it through again.

- Monitoring should tell you whether your project is or isn't on plan (page 112).
- What you monitor must be:
  - significant
  - believable
  - easy to measure and understand (page 114).

- How often you monitor must reflect the duration and risk level of your project (page 114).
- Regular monitoring keeps you in touch with your project (page 114).
- Your monitoring can use:
  - Gantt chart bars (page 116)
  - Nodes and arrows of AOA networks (page 116)
  - Nodes of AON networks (page 116)
  - Limit Testing (page 116)
  - ABC or Pareto analysis (page 117).
- Monitoring your project's cash flow is important (page 118).
- Cost monitoring can use:
  - Limit Testing (page 120)
  - ABC analysis (page 120)
  - S curves (page 121)
  - Earned Value Analysis (page 121).
- Risk monitoring is just as important as monitoring project costs and time (page 125).
- Controlling is about making sure that your project gets back to being on-course (page 126).
- Effective controlling is:
  - continuous
  - forward looking
  - very closely linked to planning (page 126).
- Your controlling can use:
  - feed-back control (page 127) and/or
  - feed-forward control (page 128).
- Your control actions need to be:
  - appropriate
  - proportionate
  - prompt and quick acting
  - cost effective

- – in opposition to causes of drift
- – based on facts – rather than opinions
- – aimed solely at keeping your project on-course (page 130).

INSTANT TIP

Efficient monitoring enables corrective action that's timely and effective. Effective controlling keeps your project on-course and on track.

07

Do you have a problem?

All projects have problems. In successful projects, these problems are identified quickly and then analysed and solved without delay. This chapter aims to help you on your way to doing that and doing it well. It looks at some of the ways in which information about your project problems can be gathered and some of the techniques that you can use to recognise, understand, analyse and, finally, solve your project problems.

Problems, problems, problems

Having a problem is an astonishingly common event. They appear everywhere – at work, home and at play. So, when you look at your project, it's not surprising to find that it, too, has its problems.

So what is a problem and why are problems so common? The typical dictionary will tell you that a problem is 'a difficult or doubtful question' or 'a situation or issue which is hard to understand or deal with'. However, when you think about these definitions and check them out against your experience, you'll soon see that they are far too generalised and broad-brush. For when it comes to the management of your ongoing project the problems that you will meet will be real and obvious. They'll act as obstacles or roadblocks. They will make movement forward difficult and they will limit your ability to achieve a desired goal or objective – such as completing an activity. These project problems will grab your attention when you become aware that there's a significant gap between what is actually happening and what you want to happen. Their basic form and nature is such that they are incomplete and unresolved; they demand an answer or solution.

But that's not the only feature or characteristic of your project problems that you need to be aware of. For problems are incredibly diverse in nature. In your project they can be about almost anything that you can think of – people, equipment, computer operating systems, the weather, suppliers, lack of information, bad planning, etc. They can range from being a well-defined problem with a single solution to being a diffuse and ill-defined problem with many possible solutions. Last, but not least, the consequences that your problems bring with them can range from those that are trivial and insignificant to those that are significant and catastrophic. Figure 7.1 illustrates the range of the characteristics of project problems.

In an ideal world, your problems – whether associated with your project or with the other parts of your life – would arrive:

- well defined
- well before they became 'critical', and
- with all the data that you needed to solve them.

But, as you know, things aren't like that in the real world. What usually happens is that problems appear:

- late
- ill defined, and
- with data that's limited or of dubious quality.

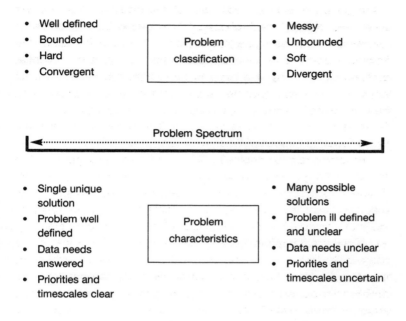

Figure 7.1: project problem spectrum

And, as if that wasn't bad enough, you'll often find that there are limited resources available to upgrade the limited information that you have got. All of this can have a significant effect upon the ways and means that you can use to try to solve your project problems.

Problem solving – the basics

Life can be difficult when you're faced with a problem in your project. The pressure is really on, you've nothing like enough information and deadlines are looming.

So what can you do? First, you need to stand back and take a good hard look at the information that you do have about your project problem. Ask yourself questions like 'Have I seen this problem before?' and 'What appear to be the problem's potential consequences?' You also need to be methodical; write down all that you know about the situation; getting, as you do, answers to the following questions:

- what is happening?
- where is it happening?
- when is it happening?

and, if you can:

- why is it happening?

When you've done that you'll probably find that the problem has changed its appearance. What had originally appeared to be a labour or productivity problem might now appear to have become a supplier or a planning problem. Getting focused like this does help. It means that the little time that you do have can now be applied in a much more focused way and by using the ways and means of project problem solving.

Project problem solving – ways

Project problem solving, at its core, is about bridging a gap – the gap between where your project's performance is and where it ought to be. As you've already seen in previous chapters, your monitoring and your project plan and budget tell you all about these two essential 'bits' of information. But they won't and can't tell you how to solve your project problem. In order to find out how to do that you've got to face your project's problems and commit yourself to the process of solving them.

However, you'll often find that you have limited time and resources available for your problem solving. When this happens, it helps if you are realistic about what you can achieve with the limited time and information that you do have available. Getting to the optimum or best solution may well be nice but it can take a lot of time and cost a lot of money. Settling for a 'good-enough' or adequate solution – even for a major problem – enables you to get the project back on track and moving forward. Doing this, as you saw in Chapter 4, is called 'satisficing'. It involves you looking through the alternative solutions to your project problem one at a time and then accepting and adopting the first one that meets a set of minimum criteria. Research tells us that doing this is a very common way of solving problems in organisations. Whether you do this or rigorously evaluate all of the options available to you to solve your problem, the process that you'll follow will be the same. This is illustrated in Figure 7.2.

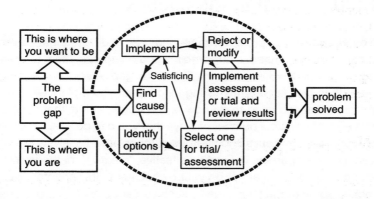

Figure 7.2: The problem solving cycle

As you can see from Figure 7.2, your problem solving process, in its fullest form, will have the following steps and stages:

- **finding** the causes of the project problem gap
- **identifying** the ways to close that gap
- **selecting** one of those for assessment or trial
- **implementing** that assessment/trial
- **reviewing** its results
- **accepting**, **rejecting** or **modifying** the option as required
- **implementing** an option.

Getting all of these right isn't just important – it's vital. It can make the difference between success and failure in your project problem solving. So let's look at each of these in turn.

Step 1: Finding the causes

You've got your project monitoring up and running. You're measuring your project's pulse-points and comparing them to what you'd planned would happen. There's a gap – you're spending more than budgeted or it's taking longer than you'd planned to do things. What you need to do now is find out what it is that causes this gap. There are a number of ways that you can do this. You can use numbers, statistics and rigorous number-based analysis or you can use less rigorous, but just as effective, 'creative' methods. You can also do it in a team or on your own. Later in this chapter you'll look at some of the techniques – such as Pareto analysis, Ishikawa diagrams and Diagramming – that you can use. Used well, these will point you towards whatever it is that's causing the gap. Doing this takes perseverance. But it isn't necessary to find out everything that's involved. As someone, somewhere, once said, 'Don't wait until you have all the answers.' It's also not necessary to overanalyse the data that you do get. The key thing to remember in this step is that you are looking for causes rather than solutions. It's also important to remember that getting all the answers and over-analysing everything will not only delay solving your problem – it'll also stop you from taking the next step in the project problem solving cycle.

Step 2: Identifying potential solutions

Now you have to identify what your options are for what might be done about that cause or causes. There are several ways of doing this. Some of them – like Brainstorming and Nominal group technique (see later in this chapter) – you may have met and used before. Others – like Force Field Analysis – may be new to you. The choice of which technique you use is up to you. But whichever technique or tool you use, you need to end up with a number of options for you do next – your future actions. You then have to decide which of these options you are going to take.

Step 3: Selecting

You're facing a choice. You've got a list of potential solutions and you have to choose one to assess or trial. When the pressure to solve your project problem and move on is high then the words and wisdom of the Japanese quality guru, Shigeo Shingo, will help. He tells you to 'think smart and think small'. What this means is that you'll be better off when you start by choosing the solution that's:

- the simplest, or
- the most efficient, or
- the most economical.

If you're going to take the 'satisficing' route – and choose the first potential solution that satisfies you – then you'll jump from this step to Step 7.

Whichever way you do it, it's worth remembering that choosing one of these alternative solutions doesn't necessarily mean that you've got the 'right' solution. There's an element of risk whichever option you choose.

Step 4: Assessment trial

This step is about exploring whether your chosen option will work; whether it will actually close the gap between where your project currently is and where you want it to be. You can do this by being analytical – using numbers, or the 'what-if' facility of your project plan, to work out the cost and consequences of the option you chose – or by undertaking a small scale trial of that option. Most of the time you'll be short on time and money so if you take the trial route then it'll need to be planned and monitored with care and forethought.

Step 5: Reviewing the results

Now that you've completed your assessment or trial of your chosen option you'll find that you're approaching a decision about what to do next. However, before you take that decision, it's worth spending a moment reviewing the results that you've generated. Questions such as these need to be asked and answered:

- did the option really, or just almost, achieve the desired result?
- if not, why not?

- are you satisfied that you've identified all the costs and consequences of the chosen option?

Step 6: Accept, reject or modify

You've reviewed the results that your assessment/trial has generated. These will tell you how well the option that you chose in Step 3 has done. If it's done well, if its performance has met or exceeded your expectations, then you'll be looking forward to using it to solve your problem. But that won't always be the case. There will be times when these results don't meet your expectations. Then you'll have to decide whether to drop that option and move on to the next one or to modify the first option and then re-assess or re-trial it. These will require you to go back to Step 4 and re-assess or re-trial the modified option, or to Step 3 to choose another option for assessment or trial.

Step 7: Implementation

You'll arrive at this step because of one of two decisions that you took earlier in the problem solving process. These were:

1. During the previous step you'll have decided to implement the solution you assessed/trialed, or
2. In Step 3 you decided to take the 'satisficing' route, chose the first potential solution that satisfied you and then jumped to this step.

Whichever route you took to get here it's worth reminding yourself about the issues that emerged in Step 4 as this implementation will also need to be planned and monitored with care and forethought.

Project problem solving – means

Now you are going to take a look at some of the many, many tools and techniques that you can use to help you to identify, define and solve your project problems. Not all of these use numbers or rational 'left brain' analytical thinking; many are based on intuitive or 'right brain' methodology. But whatever their source or methodology they are all proven and capable of helping you to solve your project problems.

Ishikawa diagrams

These diagrams – also called Fishbone or Cause and Effect diagrams – are an excellent and quickly applied method of identifying the potential causes of your problem.

To start, you draw a small box on the right-hand side of a sheet of paper in landscape or long axis horizontal orientation. In this box you write the problem or effect whose causes you want to identify. You then draw a single arrow across the sheet pointing towards the box and then add four further arrows that connect into the sides of this main arrow (see Figure 7.3). Each of these represents a group of causes as in those related to:

- people
- equipment
- method
- materials.

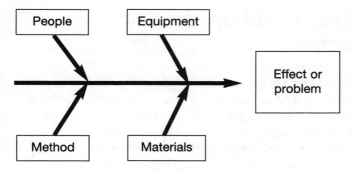

Figure 7.3: Ishikawa diagram

This basic form of the Ishikawa diagram can be extended by using Dr Ishikawa's original 5 Ms:

- Machinery
- Manpower
- Materials
- Methods, and
- Maintenance

or by adding Mother Nature to raise the count to 6 Ms.

The resulting diagram will give you a comprehensive list of all the possible causes of your problem. It will not, however, tell you which of these is the real cause. Figure 7.4 on page 144 gives you an example of an application of this technique.

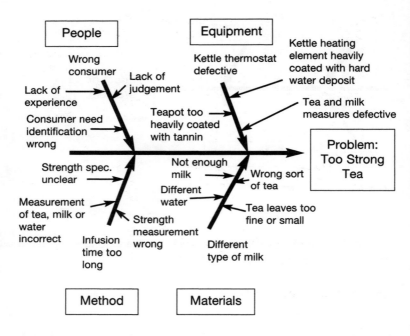

Figure 7.4: Ishikawa diagram for too strong tea problems

Diagramming

This is a simple but often underrated technique that can be used in a number of ways to help you solve your project problems. It can be used, for example, to make sure that you've identified all of the causes of a project problem (Figure 7.5).

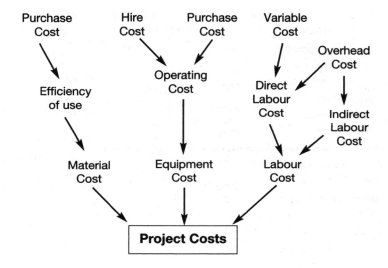

Figure 7.5: Causes of project cost diagram

Brainstorming

Brainstorming is a group technique whose aim is the generation of a large number of ideas about how your identified project problem might be solved. It has four basic rules:

1. **The more the merrier.** The assumption here is that the greater the number of ideas generated, the greater the chances are of producing a radical and effective solution.
2. **No criticism.** Criticism is put 'on hold' and contributors focus on extending or adding to an idea, rather than criticising it. The idea here is to create an open or supportive atmosphere in which contributors feel free to generate unusual or 'off-the-wall' ideas.

3. **Anything goes.** All ideas – whether bizarre, impractical or unconventional – are welcome. Ideas like this can trigger off new ways of thinking and provide better solutions than regular ideas.
4. **Combine ideas.** Ideas can be combined to form a single better idea with cross-fertilisation of ideas.

Brainstorming idea generation sessions are usually short, say half-an-hour. Ideas are spoken out loud and then written down – without being edited or censored – on a flip chart and in a numbered list that can be seen by all group members. After this session the recorded ideas are categorised by the group as:

Good
Possible
Bad, or
Unusual.

Similar ideas are then grouped together – using their numbers to identify them – and the 'Good' and 'Possible' ideas are subdivided into further categories. Each group member is then asked to pick which of the categories or ideas that they think is the most promising and to explain their choice. Each of these choices is debated within the group and a choice made of which idea(s) to proceed with. Brainstorming works best when the group is 'chaired' by a person who starts the process by identifying the problem that needs to be solved. This is written up on a sheet of paper that is placed where the entire group can see it. It's also important to have a separate person act as 'recorder'. This role writes down the ideas as they are spoken in a numbered list that can be seen by all group members. Legible handwriting and accuracy are important in this task.

Nominal group technique

This is a variation on the 'standard' brainstorming process. It aims to make sure that group members have an equal say in the process to select which idea is adopted. The outcome is a group agreement about the action that needs to be taken.

The steps of the Nominal Group process are:

1. A moderator or chairperson explains the process and rules to the group and then presents the problem. This must be done in a way that doesn't suggest a solution.
2. Working on their own, everyone writes down a list of potential solutions.
3. Everyone, in turn, reads out a single idea from their list. This is then written down on a flip chart or board. The idea creator's name is *not* recorded and the idea is *not* evaluated or criticised. This continues until all the ideas have been written down.
4. Any similar ideas are amalgamated – providing the idea generators are agreeable – and any clarification needed is given.
5. Each group member identifies their top five ideas which are then written down and given to the moderator or chairperson.
6. The moderator or chairperson amalgamates these lists and generates a top five list for the group. This is reported to the group and then discussed.
7. Finally, a similar vote is taken to identify the idea(s) to be actioned.

The moderator or chairperson will need to have been trained in the process before taking on an important problem and it may also take a few practice sessions to train the team in the process.

Lateral thinking

Lateral thinking is a way of seeking a solution to an intractable problem by using unorthodox methods that would normally be ignored by logical thinking. Identified and developed by Edward de Bono – who has written many books on its use – it involves disrupting an apparent sequence and arriving at the solution from another angle. The traditional-historical approach to problem solving, which de Bono calls 'vertical thinking', uses logic and is:

- selective
- based on judgement and proof, and
- being right or wrong.

While 'vertical' thinking looks for unique right answers, lateral thinking looks for what is different and uses information to trigger off new ideas. Chance intrusions are also welcomed.

Lateral thinking works by using the basic processes of:

- Escaping from:
  - dominant or polarising ideas
  - the prison of the 'right' answer
  - conventional entry points
  - concept 'prisons'.
- Provoking by:
  - making unjustified leaps
  - using an idea as a catalyst rather than an answer
  - separating idea generation from idea evaluation.

Lateral thinking does require training and practice to become effective but is seen by many to be highly creative in the solutions it generates. Figure 7.6 shows an example of a lateral thinking solution to a problem.

Lateral thinking

Problem: *How do you weigh an elephant?*
Solutions:

- Bury the weighing machine and let the elephant walk on it.
- Put one leg on each of four small scales.

Figure 7.6: Lateral thinking

Moving average

The moving average is a very simple but vastly underrated way of monitoring how something you're measuring moves up and down with time. You calculate it this way:

- **Step One:** Get the values for whatever it is that you're measuring for four time periods, i.e. weeks, days and months.
- **Step Two:** Add these together and divide by four. This gives you the arithmetic average value for those four periods.
- **Step Three:** When the value for the fifth period is available, add this to the previous total and then subtract the value for the first period.
- **Step Four:** Divide this new total by four. This gives you the average for periods two through to five. This is the moving average.
- **Step Five:** Continue generating these moving averages as in Steps Three and Four and plot the results you get on a graph. If you want to you can also plot the original measured values for each time period on the same graph.

The moving average is a useful and simple tool that:

- tells you whether what you are measuring is drifting up or down
- helps you to monitor what's happening
- damps or smooths out any seasonal variations or violent ups and downs that might mislead you
- requires almost no training for its use.

However, because it looks at 'smoothed' averages for a period of time, using the moving average technique may mean that you don't spot a change until some time after it has happened. If you need to make sure that this doesn't happen then use the next technique – the Cumulative sum or CuSum technique.

Cumulative sums or CuSum

The cumulative sum or CuSum technique is used to detect and identify trends or changes in measured data. It can be used, for example, to monitor trends in bricks laid per day or output per machine and gives early notice of shifts in the variable measured. It involves the comparison of measured performance data with a previously established target and the subsequent plotting of the cumulative sum of the differences. Often used as a quality control procedure, its value in project problem solving lies in its ability to detect the 'what' and the 'when' of drifts away from the project plan.

Its steps are:

1. Establish a target for what you're monitoring. This can be a desired or planned value or an historic average.
2. Subtract the first measured value from this target. The difference can be negative or positive.
3. Begin to generate the cumulative sum of these differences and start to plot this value.

4. Repeat steps 2 and 3 plotting the cumulative sum.

A simple example is shown in Figure 7.7.

CuSum plots can be used to monitor when and if one of your solutions to a problem starts to act as well as telling you what's happening in your project's key activities.

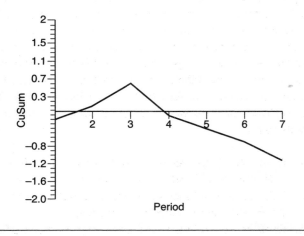

CuSum Example			
Week no.	Bricks laid (× 1000)	Difference	CuSum
1	6.2	– 0.2	– 0.2
2	6.7	+ 0.3	+ 0.1
3	6.9	+ 0.5	+ 0.6
4	5.9	– 0.5	+ 0.1
5	5.9	– 0.5	– 0.4
6	6.1	– 0.3	– 0.7
7	6.05	– 0.35	– 1.05

NOTE: Target = 6400 bricks laid/week

Figure 7.7: CuSum example

What, Where, When, Who and How

This is an analytical technique that has its roots in the Method Study methodologies that were popular in the 1960s and 1970s. Nevertheless, despite its antiquity, it does produce results.

Its steps are:

1. **What?** This initial step aims to identify what the problem is.
2. **Where?** This step aims to identify where the problem has shown itself.
3. **When?** The target of this step is the timing or sequence of the problem.
4. **Who?** This step should tell you who's involved in the problem.
5. **How?** This is about identifying how the problem occurred.
6. **Why?** This step involves repeating the first five steps but asking why? at each step. For example, why is the problem identified at step 1 a problem?
7. **What are the alternatives?** Again, this repeats the first five steps but at each step asks about alternatives. For example, at step 5 you will ask 'how else could the problem have occurred?'
8. **The way forward.** This final step repeats all five steps but decides what should be done, where it should be done, when it should be done and by whom and how it should be done.

Force Field analysis

Force Field analysis uses the point of view that says that most situations in which change is taking place can be represented as a balancing act. What are being balanced are the effects of the forces in that situation. There will be a number of these, some of which will help, promote or drive a change and others will hinder, restrain or limit that change. But this balancing act or equilibrium is not fixed or frozen – it is dynamic and interacts with the environment in which it exists. It can be portrayed by what is called a Force Field diagram.

If you want to change a situation then you must either:

- weaken one or all of the restraining forces, or
- strengthen one or all of the forces for change.

The resulting imbalance will mean that a shift or change occurs and a new equilibrium is established. The forces can be anything that acts upon or is relevant to the situation.

Force Field analysis is a simple, practical and proven way of deciding how you are going to guide, control and manage the change of solving your problem. Its steps are simple and basic and are shown below. However, the quality and effectiveness of the outcomes from this process, which can be carried out by an individual or a group, are dependent upon:

- a clear and unambiguous identification of the problem
- a detailed and comprehensive identification of the forces acting in that situation
- the presence of a practical and realistic plan for implementation.

The steps in the process are simple and obvious:

1. Identify the situation and the forces involved
2. Identify the goal
3. Decide:
   - what you're going to do, and
   - when you're going to do it.
4. Implement the above.

The implementation sequence for these actions consists of three separate though connected stages:

- unfreezing from current position
- moving to new position
- refreezing in new position.

Each of these stages must be carried through to completion if the change process is to become stable and durable.

When Force Field analysis is applied to solving your project problems the goal will be that of changing the problem situation that you find yourself in; the helping and hindering forces will be those factors that will either solve your problem or make it worse. Figure 7.8 shows a simple example.

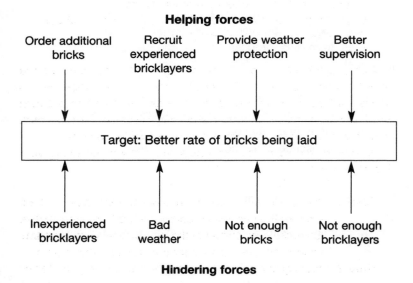

Helping forces

| Order additional bricks | Recruit experienced bricklayers | Provide weather protection | Better supervision |

Target: Better rate of bricks being laid

| Inexperienced bricklayers | Bad weather | Not enough bricks | Not enough bricklayers |

Hindering forces

Figure 7.8: Force field diagram

Pareto analysis

You've already met Pareto analysis in Chapter 6 – where you saw that you could use it when you monitor the progress of your project. But you can also use it to identify and solve your project problems. The Pareto principle says that, in any group, there are a minority of things, people or events that cause the majority of the effects or consequences. Using the empirical relationship that is often called the 80–20 or 70–30 rule you can use this sort of analysis to identify the:

- 20 or 30 per cent of activities that are responsible for 70–80 per cent of your project's labour costs, or
- 20–30 per cent of materials that are responsible for 70–80 per cent of your project's material costs, or
- 20–30 per cent of activities that account for 70–80 per cent of your project's total duration.

In your project management these effects or consequences are probably going to be about project costs or time usage. Pareto analysis will help you to identify those activities, items or problem areas in which the minimum of effort will produce the maximum gain. In short, it gives you leverage in your problem solving.

These are the steps that you need to follow when doing your Pareto analysis:

Step 1 Assemble your data. It's relative performance or effect – rather than absolute accuracy – that's important here. So make sure that all of the data you use has the same level of accuracy and is for the same period of time.

Step 2 Identify and calculate the factor that you're going to use to compare the contribution or effect of the items in your data group. You can do this by multiplying or adding or subtracting data for individual items. For example, the project cost items will be generated by multiplying usage volume by unit price while subtracting actual total costs from total budgeted costs can generate cost variance.

Step 3 Generate a table for the comparison factor of each item with the largest value at the top, the rest in descending order below.

Step 4 Calculate and add to this table the total for the comparison factor, the percentages of that total for each item's comparison factor value and the cumulative total of these percentages.

Step 5 Identify those items that lie below the 80 per cent cumulative total level in the above table. You can do this by plotting a graph of the cumulative percentages against the cumulative number or percentage of items.

These are the 20 per cent that cause the 80 per cent of the comparison factor. Having found them you'll now subject them to more detailed analysis. The object of that will be to identify and eliminate the causes of problems or weaknesses. In the example below you'll see that:

● Activities f and d account for 76.59 per cent of the total cost

● Activities f, d and g account for 89.53 per cent of the total cost.

As their contribution to project costs is some seven to nine times greater than that of the remaining items, either of these groups could be the focus of further analysis and monitoring.

Here are the steps in that example:

Steps One and Two

Activity	Unit price	Usage to date	Cost
	(£)	(000s)	(£)
a	30	2.67	80,100
b	12	4.18	50,160
c	450	0.2	90,000
d	75	20	1,500,000
e	1500	0.5	750,000
f	800	7.0	5,600,000
g	200	6.0	1,200,000

Step Three and Four

Activity	Cost	% of Total Cost	Cumulative % of Cost
	(£)		
f	5,600,000	60.41	60.41
d	1,500,000	16.18	76.59
g	1,200,000	12.94	89.54
e	750,000	8.09	97.63
c	90,000	0.97	98.60
a	80,100	0 .86	99.46
b	50,160	0.54	100.00
Total:	9,270,260		

Chapter checklist

Use the list below to check where you've got to. If you've missed something or didn't understand it go back to the page given and read it through again.

- Write down:
    - what is happening
    - where it's happening
    - when it's happening and, if you can:
    - why it's happening (page 136).

- Remember that you don't have to find the optimal solution and that satisficing will find you an 'adequate' solution (page 137).
- Make sure that you understand and use the Problem Solving Cycle (page 137).
- Your problem solving can use:
  - Ishikawa diagrams (page 142)
  - Diagramming (page 144)
  - Brainstorming (page 145)
  - Nominal group technique (page 147)
  - Lateral thinking (page 148)
  - Moving average (page 149)
  - CuSum (page 150)
  - What, Where, When, Who and How (page 152)
  - Force Field analysis (page 152)
  - Pareto analysis (page 155).

INSTANT TIP

Facing and accepting a problem is the first step towards solving it.

08

Is this the end?

The ways and means of your project closure are just as important as the ways in which you plan, launch and manage that project. This chapter looks at the how and why of project closure and tells you about the benefits of an ordered and well-organised closure. By the end of the chapter you'll have seen how a closure like this can help to ensure that your project performance is constructively and objectively assessed and evaluated. You'll also see how closing your project in this way can ensure that the lessons learnt, problems solved and techniques and tools developed are recorded and passed on for use in other projects.

At the end of the day

All projects have limited life spans and defined outcomes. As a result, they all come to a conclusion, an endpoint of one sort or another. There are no known exemptions from this natural and foreseeable event. In Chapter 1, you saw that for a successful project – one that has completed its outcome – this terminal event begins when that outcome is formally handed over. This act marks the boundary between the Adulthood and the Old Age and Termination stages of the project's life cycle.

But not all projects have such clean cut, natural and obvious endings. Some collapse, fail or are terminated early in their planned life span. For these projects, there is no project team → client handover. Their activities cease; they and their project plans are abandoned. This can happen for a variety of reasons as you'll soon see in Chapter 9. But in successful projects – particularly those that use a Client Focus or a Matrix type of project organisation – the project outcome can slip gradually, almost imperceptibly, across the boundary between being a project outcome and becoming an organisational asset. When this happens there's rarely a formal handover of any sort and the project outcome is gradually absorbed into the client organisation as it grows and develops through the Adulthood stage of project's life cycle.

However, in all of these situations, whenever they occur, the project's activities begin to slow and then, finally, stop. Despite this, there still is important work to be done. This 'end-of-the-project' work, much of which is about the fine detail of the project, possesses the potential to contribute to the success of both the project that has just closed and, just as importantly, to the next and similar projects.

Closure and the project manager

In Chapter 4 you saw that, in order to be an effective project manager, you need to be able to:

- lead
- communicate
- negotiate
- motivate, and
- take decisions.

Now, in the closing phase of your project, the demand for these skills is just as high as it has been at any time of the project's life. But the way that you use these skills will be different. For now you'll be leading and motivating a project team that's shrinking. It's also a team whose members are losing interest in the tasks that remain and are less motivated than they were in the earlier stages of the project. Some of them are anxious about whether they have post-project jobs. At the same time, the nature of your communications with the project's stakeholders will have changed. The client's senior managers will be showing less interest in the project and attending fewer project meetings. The client's operating staff will have developed an all-consuming appetite for the details of the project outcome. Throughout all of these and other changes, the business of project closure has to be carried out. As project manager you'll have to make sure that all of the outstanding outcomes, contracts and work orders are satisfactorily completed. You'll also need to negotiate the sale of some of the project's physical assets and make decisions about the disposal or storage of other assets. In all of our projects – irrespective of their size, complexity or outcomes – these and other factors combine to generate a unique and demanding set of circumstances; circumstances that demand management of a high order to ensure that the project is completed successfully. Indeed, on large or complex projects, the nature and complexity of these demands means that special project closure managers are appointed to ensure that the project reaches its end in an orderly and effective way.

Whatever the size of your project, this, the final stage of a project, represents a real challenge for you. In many ways, it's a challenge that is even greater than that which you experienced in the earlier stages of the project's life cycle. To answer this challenge you're going to have to focus on four aspects of the project's closure:

- people
- communication

- information
- power.

Let's look at each of these in turn.

Project closure and people

Projects are, as you already know, people-centred events. If your project has been successful then much of this will have been due to the way that you managed your project team. Doing this well during the project closure is just as important as it was in the earlier and more active stages of your project. One example of the way that this can be done is the creation and support of joint project team/client snag listing teams. These will audit the project outcome and then create a jointly agreed list of outstanding work or defects.

But, in the end, your project team must pass into history, just like the project that it's been such an integral and important part of. The rundown and demise of the project team needs to be managed with care. You must take into account not only the needs of team members but also the needs of the project. For the project needs to maintain, even until its last 'gasp', an effective project team. As a result you must spend time planning this project team 'wind-down'. You'll probably find that involving team members in the creation of this plan will pay dividends in terms of the commitment and performance of both the remaining and departing team members.

Project closure and communications

In Chapter 4, you saw that your project communications are important. During the course of your project these have been both formal and informal in nature and have enabled you to exchange facts, broker information, exert influence and even, on occasions, to express emotions. The primary objective of these communications has been that they should answer the information needs of the project stakeholders. As such you planned them with care and precision and made sure that they told the client about issues such as what work was in hand, what work was planned and the work that had been completed.

These needs and objectives remain the same as you approach the end of your project. Indeed, the unique pressures and difficulties of project closure increase the need for effective communication. The ways and means of this communication are the project meetings and reports that, as you saw in earlier chapters, are a regular and routine feature of the project's monitoring and control systems. The frequency of these meetings will probably increase during project closure and they will consider and review matters of detail – such as snag list team activities or work outstanding. The range and number of people who attend will also change and will now include all of the members of the smaller project team and client and stakeholder personnel involved in snag listing, commissioning, etc.

Project closure and information

By the time you reach this, the final stage of your project, a great deal of information will have been created. This will be about:

- where and on what the project money has been spent or allocated
- the detail of the outcomes that have been created, and
- how the project's resources have been consumed.

You may also have the drawings, technical specifications, operating manuals and warranties of the equipment that you've bought as part of the project and you'll certainly have the plans and programmes of project activities and copies of the contracts and sub contracts associated with the project.

If your project has a tangible outcome – such as a building or a piece of equipment – it also will have a collection of drawings, specifications and operating instructions associated with it. These will need to be transferred to the client who will need them in order to operate, maintain, repair or modify the outcome. Some of this information will need to be given to the client before the formal handover of the project outcome, so that the client's operating personnel can be trained and ready. But bringing this information about your project's outcome together isn't just an end-of-project task. This documentation needs to be acquired, organised, collated and archived from the earliest days of the project.

So what are you going to do with the rest of your project information? The answer is that you will use it to:

- identify and complete any outstanding work, and
- check that you have achieved what you set out to do.

Doing this must be planned, budgeted and managed in the same way as the other phases of your project – even when the project has failed or been terminated early in its life cycle.

Project closure and power

People who have power are able to bring about significant change, usually in other people's lives, by what they do. In our organisations people with power decide things like:

- who gets what
- when they get it, and
- how or in what form they get it.

Most of the time these people possess power because of the role or job they carry out in that organisation. But they can also be seen to be powerful because they:

- have access to or control over scarce or high value resources such as money, information or knowledge, or
- have access to other people with power or information, or
- can punish or discipline others.

As a project manager, most of your power will come from the formal role that you carry out and the control that role has over:

- project spend
- project team recruitment
- the information interchange that takes place with the client.

But you may also get some of your power from being a charismatic individual who is able to inspire your project team members and earn their trust.

However, all of this power has a definite 'use-by' date. It is only valid as long as the project is active. By the time the final stage of the project's life cycle arrives you, as project manager, will have much less power than you had in the earlier more active stages. Now you'll be operating with a much smaller project team and you'll have very limited resources left. You'll also be immersed in the fine detail of 'snag-listing' rather than the broad issues of driving the project along its track to completion.

But that's not the only change. Now, the attention of the client's senior managers will have moved away from the 'doing' part of your project and on to the problems of learning how to get the project's outcome up and running or even the problems of their next project.

It may be that both you and the client management have difficulty with all these changes. If this happens it's worth considering the introduction of a formal 'handover' ceremony. This ceremony, along with a change in your job title from 'project manager' to 'project closedown manager', will go a long way towards helping you to accept the reality of the changes in your power and responsibilities and the oncoming end of the project.

Project histories

All projects – whatever their size or outcome – are significant events. As such, they all ought to have a written history. A document that chronicles the life and times of the project, this would tell us about the project's chronology, remind us of the twists and turns of the changes in the project's plan, confirm the who did what and when of the project and tell us which procedures and systems were used.

However, for most projects, the generation of a full project history isn't justifiable. It's often seen as a luxury and its inevitable cost or the limited nature of the project militates against its creation. Under these circumstances the retrospective view that you will have of your project will be limited to that of the project audit.

Project audits

An audit is a way of evaluating something. Almost anything can be audited – an organisation, a system, a process, a project or a product. Nowadays, you can and do have safety audits, environmental audits, performance audits, and IT audits, to name but a few. The aim or objective of all of these audits is to check out the accuracy, validity and reliability of the information that's available for what's being audited. Generally, these audits aim only to provide 'reasonable' reassurance that this information is accurate and, as a consequence, random sampling – rather than 100 per cent scrutiny – is often used.

A project audit can be conducted at any point in the project's life. However, when a project is audited during the 'doing' stages of its life cycle this usually happens because of massive delays or significant overspends – performance that will have caused anxiety and concern amongst the project's stakeholders. More often than not, the project audit is conducted at the end of the project and is called a post-project or closure audit. When you undertake this audit the project actions and activities will have been completed and the project outcomes have been handed over to the client. As a result, this audit will be focused on issues such as whether any cost or plan overruns were justified and whether appropriate project management techniques were used. As the manager of the project, you will, of course, be interested in the outcomes of a closure audit. So will your client. If you both work for the same organisation then this audit is best conducted by another department of that organisation or an experienced individual employed by the organisation. If a contractor has managed the project then it's usually worth having the audit conducted by an independent third party.

All audits – whether conducted late or early in the project's life span – result in a formal report. The size, make-up and focus of this report will vary with the history, cost, duration and outcomes of the project. When large, expensive or long projects are audited, a team of mixed disciplines is usually used and the resultant report is extensive and voluminous. The audits of small or limited cost projects often result in small reports, while audits of technical sophisticated project outcomes or audits that require technically expertise – which the client may not possess – are usually conducted by independent technical experts. These reports, however, are a great deal more than bookkeeping or cost accountancy exercises. They possess the potential to reveal defects, incomplete work or defective work, any of which may be the subject of future legal action between a client and an equipment supplier or the contractor that undertook the work or managed the project.

Project appraisals

You've probably met the word 'appraisal' before. This will almost certainly have been in the context of a performance or employee appraisal – during which the performance of an employee is evaluated – or a real estate or property appraisal, during which an opinion is developed about the market value of a property. A project appraisal is, however, subtly but significantly different from either of these.

A project appraisal – or post-project appraisal as it is sometimes called – is about assessing whether the project has met the promises made when it was sanctioned. These, as you'll remember, were identified in the Conception stage of the project's life cycle and could have been about almost anything – such as sales volumes and revenues, plant or equipment performance, a new superstore or a reorganisation. Project appraisals are almost always initiated by the project client. They may, however, be conducted, for reasons of impartiality or technical content, by a third party. In large organisations with many projects and high levels of capital expenditure, post-project appraisal is often the responsibility of a dedicated department that reports to senior or board level management. These appraisals are often very comprehensive. They review the project's performance from the Conception stage of the project life cycle through to two or three years after their completion. As a result they often take several months to complete and involve a team of auditors. Their outcome takes the form of a formal, and often, substantial report.

But, despite all of this formality, a project appraisal can be productive. It can also be used to identify 'where-did-we-get-it-wrong' and 'where-did-we-get-it-right' factors of a project. As a result you may learn about the need to estimate your project costs in different ways or the need to evaluate your project risks more often. After a project appraisal you may decide that, on your next project, you'll use a different sort of project planning tool. The 'lessons' that a project appraisal can teach you can range from the fine details of the project – as in 'next time we'll hire a bigger excavator' – to the project's more fundamental issues – as in 'the need to allow a longer learning curve for new technology'. Nevertheless, these and other lessons, whatever their nature might be, come about because of the post-project appraisal.

Chapter checklist

Use the list below to check out where you are. If you've missed something or didn't understand it go back to the page given and read it through again.

- All projects come to an end because:
  - their outcome is complete, or
  - they have collapsed, failed or been abandoned (page 159).
- The project manager will still need all of his/her skills as the project draws to a close (page 161).
- Effective project closure requires the project manager to focus on four aspects of the project: people; communication; information, and power (page 161).
- People aspects of project closure need careful planning and management in order to enable the remaining tasks to be completed (page 162).
- Communication aspects of project closure will require changes in project meetings (page 162).
- Information aspects of project closure require information and documentation to be organised, collated and archived (page 163).
- Power aspects of project closure require recognition of the reality of project closure and all its implications (page 164).

- The creation of a project history is rarely justifiable (page 166).
- A project audit is usually conducted at the end of the project and aims to check out the accuracy and validity of the project's information (page 164).
- A project appraisal is about assessing whether the project has met its promises (page 168).

INSTANT TIP

In boxing, every round ends with a bell. In project management every project should end with a project audit.

09

How do you make sure your project is a success?

Success, as someone once said, is what happens when you avoid failure. At the beginning of this chapter you'll take your first step towards avoiding failure in your project by taking a look at the what, why and how often of project failure. Then you'll look at project risk and how the risks in your project can be eliminated, reduced or managed. Finally, you'll move on to find what you need to do to make sure that your project is a success.

Failure

'Failure' is one of those words that seem to get used a lot in the world of the twenty-first century. It usually surfaces when we don't carry out, complete or get something that we had planned to. When you think about it you'll soon realise that this is a pretty common experience. For example, our buses, trains or aeroplanes regularly fail to arrive or leave on time and our banks and insurance and credit card companies repeatedly fail to provide us with the level of service that they had promised.

Yet, despite all of this ubiquity, it is evident that both failure and its opposite, success, remain as significant factors in our lives. One of these – success – is desired, even lusted after, while the other – failure – is feared and viewed with trepidation. But, as you already know, these two are irretrievably connected. For it is your failures that you use to build the foundations of your next success – they teach you how *not* to do things.

So what this chapter will do first is to take at look at project failure – its nature and causes. This will be the beginning of the journey that you will take to find what you need to do to make sure that your project is a success.

Project failure – what and when

Projects, as you saw in Chapter 1, have risk – with its associated potential for both success and failure – built into their 'DNA'. They are, by nature, risky ventures. What this means is that, however well you might prepare and manage your project, it still has the potential to fail. Your project's failure can reveal itself in a number of ways.

It shows itself when, for example, you find at your project's completion that it has:

- cost more than it was budgeted to cost, or
- taken longer to complete than its planned duration, or
- generated a product or outcome that doesn't do what the original project specification said it would do.

When you get any one or more of these happening in your project it means that, for one reason or another, your project has failed to achieve its desired endpoints. These are the endpoints that, as you saw earlier in this book, were defined at your project's sanction point and should have been defended and protected during your project's life span.

But this isn't the only way that a project can fail. Projects can also collapse before their scheduled endpoint. When this occurs they fail to complete. This can happen for a variety of reasons. It happens when, for example, the project's planned but yet-to-be-achieved outcome becomes obsolete or gets overtaken and swept away by a 'bigger-and-better' alternative. It can also happen when your project's prototype outcome fails, when your project's cost or schedule run out of control or when the senior executive project champion falls by the corporate wayside. As you saw in Chapter 8, for these projects there is no project team/client handover to mark their end. They are terminated, prematurely, and then abandoned or dumped in the corporate 'ashcan'.

But when you think about all of these and the other project failures that you might have seen or experienced you'll soon see that project failure isn't a black or white affair. For there are degrees of failure. In fact, it can be argued that what exists is a failure/success spectrum that has at each of its ends the absolute versions of project success and project failure as shown in Figure 9.1.

What you can see here is the success/failure spectrum, at one end of which lies Absolute Project Failure – as when projects are terminated early and incomplete. At the other end lies Absolute Project Success – as when projects are completed to budget, plan and specified scope. In between these extremes you get projects that fail to meet one, two or three of the defined dimensions of cost, time and scope. These are often called damaged or injured projects rather than failed projects. Nevertheless, it is worth noting that, in terms of their initial definitions of duration, cost and outcome, these projects have failed.

So let's move on now to see if you can find out why these failures occur and how often that happens.

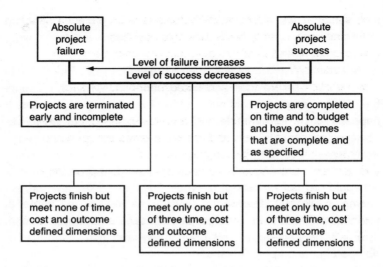

Figure 9.1: Success/failure spectrum

Project failure – how often and why

Unfortunately, when you do move on to find out why projects fail, you'll soon hit a stumbling block. This is because there aren't many comprehensive studies of project failure. There are many reasons for this, including potential, actual or pending lawsuits, corporate reputations, and last, but not least, embarrassment. However, what information that there is does give you some pretty strong hints as to why projects fail.

One example of this is the list of common causes of project failure produced by the UK Government's National Audit Office. This tells you that most projects fail because of:

- the absence of a clear link between the project and the client organisation's key strategic priorities
- lack of clear senior management ownership and leadership
- lack of connection to and engagement with project stakeholders
- lack of project management and risk management skills
- project development and implementation stages not broken into manageable steps
- projects chosen on initial price or cost rather than long-term value for money
- supply side problems
- lack of integration between project team, stakeholder and suppliers.

Other studies tell us that the major reasons for project failure are far more basic:

- poor project definition
- unclear objectives
- unrealistic targets
- inadequate risk evaluation
- client inexperience
- poor forecasting of demand
- lack of an effective sponsor and strong leadership
- poor communication and lack of openness
- inadequate stakeholder management
- management focus wrongly targeted at the back end.

By now you've probably realised that almost all of the causes of project failure in this list could have been eliminated by the use of good project management practice at the front end or very early stages of a project.

When you come to look for information about how often projects fail you'll find that most of the project failure studies that are accessible have looked at failed information technology (IT) or management information system (MIS) projects. The picture that emerges from these studies is not a good one. Using the definitions of failure and success that you saw in Figure 9.1, it seems that, on average, in any ten typical IT or MIS projects:

- only two or three will succeed
- a further four or five will finish damaged or injured in some way
- between two and three will completely fail.

There are, of course, many views about why these extraordinarily high levels of project damage and failure occur. Nevertheless, when you wade through these, a consensus does seem to emerge. This tells you that significant amongst the causes of project damage and failure are issues such as:

- lack of client or user involvement
- inadequate or changing outcome specifications
- lack of senior management support
- inadequate or absent planning
- project management incompetence
- outcome is obsolete on completion
- inadequate or inefficient communication
- inadequate risk management.

It could be argued that some of these – such as project outcome obsolescence – are peculiar to IT projects. But you don't have to be a genius to see that many of the other causes – such as shifting outcome specifications, lack of planning, poor project management and lack of communication – are about issues and processes that are core to the business of project management. As such they reveal very basic flaws in the way that these projects were managed.

Project failure – evasion and eradication

By now it should be clear that, for all of these and sometimes other reasons, your project has the potential to fail and fall by the wayside. Nobody is happy when this happens – you certainly won't get a medal if it takes place and it's not, at all, what you had planned or hoped for.

So what can you do to make sure that these sorts of thing don't happen? How can you, for example, make sure that your project doesn't suffer from such basic defects as:

- project planning that isn't 'up to the job'? or
- a project outcome specification that isn't defended? or
- a failure to communicate with clients or users?

If you step back and take a long look at these questions you'll soon see that the answers to them are quite obvious. In the earlier chapters of this book you have seen what the key steps of effective project management are. You've seen, for example, how important it is to plan your project in a thorough and professional way and how absolutely necessary it is to generate an accurate and valid project specification and then rigorously defend that project specification throughout your project's life cycle.

So, if you want to make sure that your project does not fall victim to these failure causes then you must make sure that you manage it in ways that are proficient, professional and to the highest possible standards. There is no room for short-cuts or bypasses on the road to project success. If your project is going to be a success then, whatever the pressure, you're going to have to resist the temptation to lower your standards or assume 'it'll be all right' when you're faced with a problem or setback.

But even when you manage your project well, it can still contain the potential to fail. It will still be vulnerable to the 'slings and arrows of outrageous fortune'. As Murphy's Law tells us, 'Whatever can go wrong will go wrong, and at the worst possible time, in the worst possible way'. As a result, things can still go wrong – unpredictably and sometimes disastrously. You've already seen that in order to anticipate, monitor and manage those sorts of situations you need to have and use an effective risk management system. When you've got one of these you will, in the early days of your project, have:

- evaluated (Chapter 10) the risk of these and other things happening
- built additional 'float' or contingency time into your plan (Chapter 3)
- monitored the remaining risks (Chapter 6) and
- added a contingency allowance to your project cost estimate (Chapter 10).

So let's take a look at how this process of risk evaluation and management begins.

Risk and uncertainty

Risk is an ever-present factor in all of our lives. It's there all the time, whatever we do, as is its close relative, uncertainty. However hard we try to order and control our lives there will always be events and choices that we hadn't foreseen and information that wasn't available when we needed it. All of these combine to create risk.

Our projects are no exception to this. They are, as you've already seen in Chapter 1, risky ventures. So, despite the fact that you can and will plan and manage your projects to the highest professional standards, your projects can never be 'risk-free'. What you can do, however, is to act to reduce or limit the influence that risk exerts on your project. When you do this you not only increase the project's chances of success, you also increase your ability to manage that project effectively.

In order to do this you need to take the following steps:

1. Identify the source and nature of each foreseeable risk.
2. Reduce that risk or, if possible, eliminate it.
3. Decide whether or not you will accept the risk that remains.

Completing and continuing to use this three-stage sequence is a must for all projects. Without it your project is at risk of failure. So let's look at each of these steps in turn:

1. Risk identification

In this, the initial step of your risk management process, you need to discover or uncover the nature and source of your project's risks. The risk matrix (Figure 9.2) is a good way of starting that process. This matrix tells you that if your project has an outcome that has been successfully achieved in the past – as in 'been done before' – and that the methods that you intend to use to achieve that outcome are well proven – also as in 'been done before' – then the project is low risk. If, however, either of those factors change to 'never been done before' then the risk level of the project will rise. Using this matrix provides you with a quick and easy way of establishing the risk level of your project. It can also, of course, be applied to individual elements or activities of your project, thus giving you a more detailed assessment of the project's risks

Project outcome	Project change process: Been done before	Project change process: Never been done before
Been done before	Low Risk	Medium Risk
Never been done before	Medium Risk	High Risk

Figure 9.2: Project risk matrix

You can also use the two Cs – Cause and Consequence – to identify your risks. For you can:

- look at the causes of a risk event and then at its consequences – as in what might happen and what would then follow if it did happen?; or
- look at the risk event's consequences and then at its causes – as in what is an undesirable outcome and how might it be caused?

In the first of these – looking initially at a cause and then at consequences – you'll ask 'What happens if the bricks (to build that wall) aren't delivered on time?' You'll then identify and list the consequences, such as delay or non-completion of the wall and delay to or non-completion of the subsequent tasks that depend upon the wall being finished. In the second of these analyses, the one that looks at consequences first and then identifies the possible causes, you'll start by asking something like 'What might cause you to be unable to build that wall?' You'll then go on to list the possible causes: both direct, as when the bricks aren't delivered on time; and indirect, as when the excavation of the wall's foundation was delayed by bad weather. In this stage you'll generate, first, a description of the risk – such as supplier not meeting delivery deadline, and then, second, a description of its impact – such as milestones not achieved. These two then give you a definition of your risk, such as 'vendor not meeting deadline will mean that programmed float will be exceeded'.

But, as you already know, just identifying the nature and source of your project's risks isn't enough. You actually need to do something about them.

2. Risk reduction or elimination

Now that you know what your project's risks are, the next step in your risk management process is for you to come up with an estimate about how likely these risk events are to happen. This won't be a 'yes-or-no' estimate but one that tells you or reflects the fact that some risk events will be more (or less) likely to happen than others. But you won't necessarily need a lot of complicated statistics. Each risk can be rated simply – on a scale of 1 to 4, the larger the number the higher the likelihood of that event happening. Use all the sources of information that you can, including project appraisals (Chapter 8), brainstorming (Chapter 7) and other people's experience. The level and amount of information that you need to make these failure estimates will depend upon two factors:

- the nature of the material or hardware involved, and
- the project's position in its life cycle.

If, for example, you are looking at the risk of a piece of equipment or hardware failing, then there are databanks that will tell you how likely this event is. These will give you, for example, a specific and detailed figure for the mean time before failure (MTBF) of a particular piece of equipment or hardware. But if you're in the earliest part of the Conception phase of the project's life cycle, the objectives of the project will have been expressed only in broad and general terms and a low level of detail will suffice. Later, when you get to end of this stage – when a project is sanctioned and comparisons are being made with other projects – a higher level of detail will be needed.

Once you've arrived at this estimate of the likelihood of a risk event happening then you've got to decide what you're going to do to reduce or even eliminate that risk. If you do this for the wall-building example above then you'll probably conclude that brick deliveries are routine events with a low likelihood of failure. But you may want to reduce that likelihood of failure to an even lower level by making sure that the order is confirmed two weeks before the delivery date and ringing up the supplier on the day before delivery is due. But there are other things that you can do. For example you can:

- avoid the risk or do something to remove it such as using another or several suppliers.
- transfer the risk or make someone else responsible, such as making a subcontractor guarantee his or her performance.
- accept the risk, particularly if it or its consequences are small.

Once you have done all of this then you're in a position to decide whether or not you can live with, even accept, your project's risks.

3. Yes or no?

You've reached the point where you've identified the source, nature and level of your project risk and done what you can to reduce it. Now you've got to make a decision – about whether or not you can tolerate that risk. A risk analysis log (Figure 9.3) can help you to make that decision as it enables you to review each of your project's risks and rate them against each other.

Risk Analysis Log
Score risk likelihood and impact as follows:
High = 3, Medium = 2, Low = 1

Risk	Likelihood rating	Impact rating	Likelihood x impact [score]	Actions required	Person responsible

Figure 9.3: Risk analysis log

What's also going to help you is the fact that you will continue to monitor these risks (see Chapter 6) in order to pick up any changes or additions.

Project success – the way forward

Project failures are expensive, frustrating and stressful events that should be avoided at all costs. But, by now, you should have realised that there aren't any instant solutions or 'silver bullets' to help you to do that. Despite this you'll find that the literature of project management is rich in views about how to make sure that you achieve success in your projects. Some of these are effective, others aren't; some reflect real wisdom and experience while others owe more to academic theory that real practice. In the end, the choice of what you do to avoid failure and ensure success in your project is up to you. By now you should be well along the road towards having enough knowledge to start or even extend your project management career. So it'll be your 'home-cooked formula', rather than someone else's theories, that will work for you. Nevertheless there are some things than are worth sharing with you. So here, in Figure 9.4, they are.

The Key Steps to Project Success

1. Start with:
   - a clearly defined project specification
   - a competent project manager and project team
   - support from senior management
   - sufficient resources (money, equipment, etc.)
   - a planning system that you are comfortable with.

   Don't start until you have all of the above – you'll be wasting your time if you do!

2. Work hard to develop and use:
   - a team that works and solves problems together
   - a plan that works and is responsive to change
   - a communication system that reaches the right people.
   - a good, open and responsive relationship with client/user/stakeholders
   - an effective change control that defends the project specification that you started with
   - an efficient control and monitoring system that keeps you on course.

3. Complete your project with:
   - an outcome that's on time, within budgeted cost and meets the project specification
   - a project history, audit or appraisal that will help you, next time, to get it 'right first time'.

Figure 9.4: The key steps to project success

Chapter checklist

Use the list below to check out where you've got to. If you've missed something or didn't understand it go back to the page given and read it through again.

- Failure and success are common factors in all of our lives (page 171).
- All projects have the potential to fail (page 172).
- Absolute project success and absolute project failure lie at opposite ends of a failure spectrum and there are degrees of project failure (page 173).
- There are many views about why projects fail (page 173).
- Most IT projects seem to fail or finish damaged in some way (page 176).
- Thorough professional project management is key to your project's success (page 177).
- Managing your project risk reduces your project chance of failing (page 178).
- Project success follows when you manage your project well and with confidence (page 184).

INSTANT TIP

Project success follows when project managers manage risk and make the time to do things right.

10

Which project will you do?

Selecting the 'right' project is a key first step in the management of a successful project. Making that choice – about which of many projects to put your efforts into – isn't an easy one. This chapter takes a look at the way that's done. By the time you get to its end, you'll be much clearer about how to get the information that you need, and how to make that choice.

In the beginning

You've arrived at the start of this, the final chapter in this book, for one of two reasons. Either:

- you've finished your first project and now face a choice about the next project that you manage, or
- you're faced with a choice about which project you choose to start your journey to becoming a successful project manager.

But, whichever way you've got here, the route that you'll follow from here – to choosing your project – will be the same. And it's a route that starts with a search for information about that project.

Getting it together

In Chapter 1, you saw that all projects have:

- an outcome
- a defined length of time that's needed to achieve that outcome
- a total cost of the resources that will be used.

You also saw that these dimensions – outcome, time and cost – don't stand alone. You cannot, for example, reduce the time span of a project without taking into account the effect that has upon both the project outcome and the cost of the project. Nor can you trim the budget of your project without considering and probably changing the time needed to complete that project or the nature of the project's outcome.

Now, faced with making a choice about your next (or first) project, you'll need to make sure that you've got enough information about these, the dimensions of your potential project. You'll need to do this both before and during the process that will lead you to a decision about your project. This is the process that, as you saw in Chapter 1, takes place in the initial or Conception stage of your project's life cycle. It's a process with two steps or stages: first, you choose the project that you want to support and then, second, that project competes with other projects for sanction. But doing all of that isn't as difficult as it might seem.

You now need to start to create the first version of the Project Specification or Project Initiation Document (PID) (see Chapter 2) for your potential project. When completed this should tell the reader about the project's:

- name or title and reference number (if any)
- justification, objectives and deliverables
- expenditure and timetable
- organisation.

However, at this moment in time, you'll probably only be able to write in what the name of the project is, what its aims, objectives and outcome are and what its target completion date or duration is. Stating these accurately, briefly and correctly, is important as, after you've chosen the project that you want to support, this document will move on to be extended to contain the information required for the step of choosing which project is sanctioned. Once your project is approved or sanctioned, this document becomes a baseline against which project progress is assessed and requested changes assessed.

This document can also be used as a start point for the process of creating the initial version of your project plan. But in order to move on from this start point you'll need some more information about your embryonic project, such as:

- what actions and activities must be completed if you need to reach those goals and objectives within the given time span?
- when do these actions need to take place?
- how many people will you need and with what skills?
- what sort of equipment, tools and materials will you need?

The answers to these questions, however limited they might be, provide the basis of your potential project's first Work Breakdown Schedule (WBS). This document is the foundation stone of your first project plan and Figure 10.1 shows an example of an early stage WBS.

Vending Machine Project
Work Breakdown Schedule

Phase 1: Activity areas

- Select and supply machine
- Selection of location
- Provision of electrical power
- Provision of potable water
- Provision of waste water drainage
- Provision of storage for consumables
- Provision of solid waste facilities – cups etc.

Figure 10.1: Vending machine project WBS

In order to estimate how long it will take to complete these activities you'll need to tap into a number of sources of information. For example, on the vending machine project above, the vending machine manufacturers will be able to give you information about what needs to be done and how long that will take. You may also find that other people have done some or all of the activities involved in your embryonic project before. However, if uncertainty levels remain high you can, as you saw in Chapter 3, use the following formula:

Expected duration = $(a + 4m + b)/6$
Where a = optimistic duration
        b = pessimistic duration
and   m = most likely duration

But, if your embryonic project takes you beyond the boundaries of your prior experience or easily accessible information, then get professional help.

Using a Gantt or bar chart (see Chapter 3) for this plan will provide enough detail at this stage – but do make sure that you keep records of all the information that you have used to generate that plan together with the assumptions you made in getting to that information. You will need all of this later in the process when you come to expand your plan or if you decide to shift your planning into an Activity on Arrow or Activity on Node network.

At this stage, however, it's worth keeping your plan simple and straightforward with a timescale based on units of days for a small project and weeks for a larger one. You don't, at this time, need to know the fine detail of your potential project.

Finally, when you've completed these initial versions of your embryonic project's WBS and plan, you'll need to generate a cost estimate for your potential project. This is a process that you'll now look at in more detail.

Guesstimates and estimates

Cost estimating is not an exact science. Nevertheless, identifying the money needs of a potential 'next project' is a vitally important part of the process for choosing what project you're going to do next. Get it wrong and it won't matter how well you've planned your project's activities or defined your project's outcome – because that project will fail. Get it right and your project will come to life and begin its journey to success.

The project estimate is the first step towards doing that. This estimate will be used in a number of ways. In these, the early days of your potential project, it will help you to answer questions such as 'Is this new product worth further investigation?' or 'Is this book worth publishing?' Later, it will be used in the process of deciding which of a number of competing projects represents the best investment for the funds of your organisation. Finally, once your project has been approved, this estimate becomes the core of the project's budget – a budget that's used in the process of monitoring and controlling the project. But each of these tasks has different needs. For example, an initial cost estimate with a low level of accuracy will be adequate to find out whether the idea of a project is worth further investigation, while a higher level of accuracy will be needed when it comes to deciding which project is sanctioned. These, typically, are the levels of accuracy relevant to the stages of the project's journey from idea to outcome:

Stage	Typical description	% accuracy
Preliminary decision taking	'seat of the pants', 'ball-park', 'order of magnitude' estimate	± 50%
Go/no go decision	Sanction estimate	± 10%
Activities begin	Definitive or Project Control estimate	± 5 to 10%

But, whatever their accuracy levels, it is important that these estimates are generated by the exercise of skill and judgement and using the best information available at the time of their creation. This can come from a variety of sources including previous projects, quotations from suppliers and contractors, cost engineering consultants and, last but not least, reference books.

In the early part of your project's life cycle – when levels of accuracy as low as ± 50% are acceptable – 'top-down' estimating methods can be used. These start from information that contains the lowest level of detail about the project, such as a statement about the size of the project – as in a 200,000 m^2 warehouse, a 200-page book, 100 t/day ammonia plant – or the size and cost of its most significant item. When you use the size of the project outcome to generate your cost estimate you'll use what's called the exponential method. In this you calculate the cost of the new project by using the following equation:

Cost of new project = Cost of old project $\times (S_{new}/S_{old})^{0.66}$

where S_{new} = size or capacity of your new project
S_{old} = size or capacity of old project.

The exponents used will depend on the nature of your project but usually lie in the range 0.6 to 0.75. When you are using this method you need to ensure that you are comparing like with like and remember that the accuracy of the result is as low as ± 50%.

The second of the top-down methods that you can use is called the factorial or parametric estimating method. This starts from a detailed and accurate cost for a core item in the project outcome, such as a boiler in a boiler house project or a vending machine in a drinks vending machine project. This core cost is then used to find the cost of the other bits of the project, such as piping, electrical services, foundations, etc. For example, when the cost of a vending machine is £2,000, you can estimate that the cost of the water supply might be (£2,000 × 0.12) = £240 and the cost of the electrical services might be (£2,000 × 0.08) = £160. Add all these together and you arrive at the total cost. There are a number of sources of these factors. When you are using this method you need to be sure that the factors are developed from a database that is relevant, accurate and large enough.

As the level of accuracy needed for your estimate rises you'll make the shift into using 'bottom-up' estimating methods. These use the information contained in your project's Work Breakdown Schedule (WBS). The greater the level of detail in this schedule, the higher the level of accuracy of the estimate and the highest level of WBS detail exists in the final and definitive version that's contained in the project specification.

Whatever the level of accuracy, the information used has to be both realistic and well founded and reflect issues like learning curves and the reality that work rates start low, rise, and then fall. The resultant estimates must also take into account 'above-the-line' costs such as equipment hire and indirect costs such as the salary costs of the project manager, secretaries, clerks, etc. They must also include 'below-the-line' costs such as design charges from outside agencies, consultancy fees, inspection fees, the costs of insurance and an allowance for inflation. Last, but not least, your estimate must include a contingency allowance (usually 5 per cent of total project estimate) which will reflect the risk level or novelty of your project and act as a hedge against things like unknown or difficult-to-predict events.

Generating an estimate is a complicated task and one that, by its nature, attempts to anticipate the future costs of events. It involves risk and uncertainty and these can lead to your project's failure. But risk (see Chapter 9) can be managed. In order to do that you need to take the following steps:

1. Identify the source and nature of each foreseeable risk.
2. Reduce that risk or, if possible, eliminate it.
3. Decide whether or not you will accept the risk that remains.

Completing this three-stage sequence is a must for the process of project selection. Without it the projects that you select will be doomed to failure. You also need to make sure that your estimate is as comprehensive as it needs to be by using the Estimate Checklist shown in Figure 10.2.

Choosing

Once you've got all the information that you need you'll be ready to get into the choosing bit of the process that sits at the core of the conception stage of your project's life cycle. There are two parts to this. First, you choose what project you are going to support and then second, that project competes with other projects to be considered for sanction.

Project Estimate Checklist

Does your project estimate include:

1. Overheads such as:
   - design fees?
   - consultancy fees?
   - insurance costs?
2. Labour costs such as:
   - project manager/team costs?
   - direct labour costs?
   - sub contract labour costs?
   - temporary labour cost?
3. Material cost such as those needed for:
   - services supply, such as electricity, water, gas heating and ventilation?
   - any building work?
   - special materials?
4. Equipment costs such as costs for equipment:
   - purchase?
   - lease?
   - rental?
5. Contingency allowance?
6. Inflation allowance?

Figure 10.2: Project estimate checklist

The first stage is a relatively straightforward one. It's a choice that should always be decided in a rational, conscious and formal manner. You'll probably take that decision on your own and you will probably choose and give your support to a project that:

- gives the quickest and highest return on invested capital, and
- involves the lowest risk.

But when you move up to the second stage – the 'which-project-gets-sanctioned?' stage – then life can, and often does, get a little more complicated. For example, if you work in an unusually profitable organisation you may find that it will be prepared to spend on speculative high risk projects, while an organisation with lower profits would not. Similarly, you'll probably find that a non-profit-making organisation will fund projects that increase the effectiveness of its use of scarce or expensive resources, such as capital or people, while a profit-making organisation will be concerned only with levels of profitability. The capital available for projects can also vary. It might be a fixed amount – resulting in intense competition between projects, or an unlimited amount – resulting in all projects whose marginal cost equals their marginal return being funded. Usually, however, demand for capital outweighs the amount available. As a result your estimate of the capital needs of your project can be crucially influential as to whether it is, or isn't, sanctioned. The factors that influence the choice of which project gets sanctioned are diverse and various. They include legislation, interest rates, the actions of competitors, the current industrial relations climate and, most important of all, whether the project has a strong business case that supports the organisation's business plan or strategy. Not the least of these influences are the interests and needs of the project stakeholders who, as we saw in Chapter 1, all have something to gain or lose by the way that the decision about their particular project turns out.

In large organisations, the decision as to which project to sanction is often taken by several senior managers acting in a group that is sometimes called a 'capital investment committee' or 'sanctioning committee'. However, its title can reflect the outcome of the projects, as in the 'publishing committee' of a book publisher or the 'new products' group of a detergent manufacturer. In smaller organisations the company owner or the organisation's general manager often takes the sanction decision.

The techniques that are used to help with this decision are both numerical and non-numerical in nature. You can, for example, make your choice on the basis of which project takes the shortest time to pay back the initial capital investment or by using sophisticated accounting concepts such as Net Present Value. You might also use non-numerical techniques that allow you to exercise or express your intuition or preferences. All of these techniques are versatile enough to be used in a wide variety of situations. But in all of these situations each of the alternative projects will have different costs, different benefits and dissimilar risks. None of these will be known with absolute certainty. But all of this risk and uncertainty are, together with many other factors, brought to bear upon your choice of which project to implement – a choice that is, as you saw earlier, a key step in the process of managing a successful project.

Choosing without numbers

There will always be projects that arise or appear without enough supporting information. This might happen, for example, when you need to react quickly to circumstances or when the information just isn't available and won't be for the foreseeable future. When this happens you need to evaluate the project on a subjective rather than an objective basis. Some examples of when and how this is done are as follows:

Hurricanes, floods, tornadoes and other events

When your factory, shop, or office is threatened by an oncoming storm, flood, tornado or hurricane you need to do something about it – and quickly. This may, for example, involve buying storm shutters or boards to protect your office block, building a protective dyke to divert flood water away or buying sand for sand bags. When this sort of thing happens a formal project evaluation is not only impractical, it's also irrelevant. What does help, however, is asking yourself – and answering – simple questions such as 'Is the factory worth protecting, and if so, at what cost?' Of course, it will be worth protecting but the question will make you think about how much money you are prepared to spend when faced with what appears to be an imminent catastrophe. When damage does occur then the question changes to 'Is the factory or office worth repairing, and if so, at what cost?' A 'no' answer means that you need to create a new project for a replacement facility. If the answer is yes, that is, that you do need to repair the damage in order to stay in business, then the focus of the project's control will be on the required current expenditure rather than on meeting a non-existent budget. However, even this expenditure must have its limits, the most obvious being that you wouldn't spend more in repair costs than the value of the shop or factory.

Legal must-dos

All governments, state legislatures and federal agencies generate laws, codes, statutory rules and regulations. These are aimed at telling you and I what we can and cannot do in our organisations and homes. They are often subject to change or reinterpretation.

As a consequence the ways in which you operate your business and what you do in your place of work may also have to change. These are often mandatory projects – you have little choice about whether you do, or don't, implement them. As a result, the management of this type of project is focused on the control of the required expenditure. Examples of this sort of project might include the provision, in public places, of access for the disabled, installing ventilation equipment to limit employees' exposure to fumes or the provision of wrist supports or special keyboards to prevent RSI (Repetitive Strain Injury).

Canteens and car parks

Some projects are about such things as staff canteens, sports facilities or car parking facilities. These are called employee welfare projects and are generally created, sanctioned and implemented as a result of an organisation's human resources policy. They rarely, if ever, generate a financial return of any sort and can involve high levels of capital spend. They do, nevertheless, require careful management, monitoring and control.

Sacred cow projects

These projects come about because of the power and influence of senior managers. They can have beginnings that are as modest as the CEO (Chief Executive Officer) asking 'Why don't we have a look at ...', or that are as complex as an individual manager's need to prove their suitability for a more senior role by his or her patronage of projects with a rapid effect on profit. Their selection is almost always surrounded with 'political' intrigue and might, under extreme circumstances, bypass the formal project selection procedures. The best advice that could be given about these projects is to avoid any contact with them. However, a select and 'very-difficult-to-spot' minority of these will reflect the inspired intuition or 'gut feel' of experienced, capable and powerful managers.

Competitive advantage

Today's business environment is fiercely competitive and often very volatile. Competitive advantage or 'catching the top of the market' can, and does, make a significant and very positive contribution to an organisation's profitability. A project that has this potential needs to be sanctioned quickly so that it can enter the marketplace ahead of any rival. These 'fast-track' projects are not without their risks – risks that could be reduced by feasibility studies or prototyping. Nevertheless, once sanctioned, they do need careful management and control.

Ranking

Comparative ranking is a technique that can be used to help you to choose between a number of similar projects. Used when you have limited or even no quantitative information about a number of projects, it will rely on your ranking these projects, relative to each other, under a number of headings. The project with the best total ranking is then chosen for implementation. The headings chosen must reflect the nature of these projects but must be equally applicable to all of them. For example, a comparison between different sites for a new factory should have headings for road and rail access, labour availability, ease of construction and availability of utilities. Similarly, a comparison between different sorts of delivery vehicle might use headings for capital cost, maintenance cost, insurance cost, ease of parking, load-bearing capacity and fuel costs. A ranking matrix is used to compare the alternative projects, using the relative ranking, for say three projects, of 1 being the best and 3 being the worst. The overall best of these alternatives will then have the lowest total score.

This sort of process is quick and easy to use, mainly because of its need for 'better or worse than' assessments rather than absolute numbers.

Choosing by numbers

Money is a scarce but vital commodity in the world of projects. As a result, your potential projects are often evaluated, reviewed and chosen by the use of numerical methods.

Examples of how this can be done include the following.

Payback period method

A project's payback period is the length of time that it takes for the project outcome to repay its initial capital investment. Projects with short payback periods are attractive propositions and are often chosen in preference to those with longer payback periods. Payback period is a simple and easy-to-use method which is appropriate for low-cost projects. For example, a project with a completion cost of £200,000 and an annual profit of £45,000 will have a payback period of £200,000/£45,000 or 4.4 years

But don't use it on high-cost or long time span projects – as it assumes that cash flows after the payback period are of no interest or that money doesn't change in value as time passes.

Rate of return method

A project's rate of return (ROR) is the ratio of money gained or lost on the project to the amount of money invested in it. Often also called return on investment (ROI), it's usually expressed as a percentage figure, and is calculated by dividing the annual profit by the implementation cost. The project with the highest rate of return is the one that is chosen.

In the example given above the rate of return is calculated as follows:

Annual profit/Implementation cost = 45,000/200,000 = 22.5%

A simple and easy-to-use method, that is best applied to low-cost, short time-scale projects, ROR generates an average rate of return for the period considered. It also assumes that the value of money doesn't change with time.

Net Present Value (NPV) or Discounted Cash Flow (DCF) method

Discounting is the process that you use to find the present value of future earnings. It's the opposite of compounding, which finds the future value of present earnings. The discounted value of these earnings is calculated by reducing its value (using the appropriate discount rate) for each period of time that passes between now and when those earnings were generated. Discount rates are usually expressed as annual rates and the present values are calculated by dividing them by one plus the interest rate for each year that will pass. When you use discounting in your project selection process it means that you can ignore factors like the changing values of the project's goods and equipment. DCF or NPV allows for the fact that the value of money does change with time by converting all of the future earnings of a project to their present-day value.

NPV is calculated as follows:

Net Present Value = [Future value cash flow total/(1 + interest rate) ^{n}] – Capital invested

where n is the number of years.

Values of $1/(1+ \text{interest rate})^n$ can be found in books of discounting tables.

This means that for a project with an assumed interest rate of 10%, an implementation cost of £3,000 and forecast profit pattern of £1,600, £1,500, £1,400 and £1,800 in years 1, 2, 3 and 4 respectively, you can calculate its net present value like this:

Year number	1	2	3	4
Value of $1/(1+r)^n$	.9091	.8264	.7513	.6830
Annual Profit (£)	1,600	1,500	1,400	1,800
Present Value of Annual Profits (£)	1,454.6	1,239.6	1,051.8	1,229.4

The total present value of these annual profits is £4,975.4, which exceeds the implementation cost of £4,000 by £975.4. This tells you that, if this project is implemented, the value of the organisation will increase. Projects with this sort of result are seen as good risks and get sanctioned. But if the sum of these discounted future cash flows or present values of forecast profits is less than the implementation cost of the project then it should be rejected, as the value of the organisation will fall.

Profitability Index

The Profitability Index – sometimes called the Benefit–Cost Ratio – is the ratio of the sum of the net present values of forecast profits to the capital required for implementation. If the value of this ratio exceeds 1.0 then the project is acceptable. The higher the value is, the more acceptable the project is. In the example given above, the Profitability Index would have been £4,975.4/£4,000 or 1.243.

Internal Rate of Return (IRR)

This method of assessing whether or not projects are suitable for investment also uses the NPV of the project. But, unlike the NPV, which indicates value or magnitude, the internal rate of return tells you about the efficiency of the potential project investment. The IRR is calculated by discounting the future annual profits of the project over a range of interest rates and then calculating the NPV (for a given period of time) at each of those rates. What happens is that the NPV falls as the interest rate rises. The interest rate at which the NPV becomes zero is called the Internal Rate of Return (IRR). The higher the interest rate is, the better the project. But, in the end, the choice of whether or not to sanction a project is based on whether this Internal Rate of Return exceeds the cost to the organisation of borrowed capital. If the IRR exceeds this rate then the project should be sanctioned. If it is below this borrowing cost, then the project should be rejected.

Chapter checklist

Well done! Again, you've covered a lot of ground in this chapter. Use the list below to check out where you've got to. If you've missed something or didn't understand it go back to the page given and read it through again.

- Getting to your next project has two steps:
  1. Choosing the project that you want to support.
  2. Submitting that project for sanction (page 188).
- To complete both of these steps you're going to have to put together or generate information about the potential project's: outcome; time span; total cost (page 188).
- The scope and accuracy of this information will increase as the project moves through the initial Conception phase of its life cycle (page 189).

- Your project cost estimates will change from the 'ballpark' level (± 50%) to the Sanction estimate level (±10%) (page 191).
- If your project is sanctioned it will need a project control estimate (± 5 to 10%) (page 192).
- Your cost estimates can be generated by using:
  - top-down methods such as the exponential or parametric methods (page 192).
  - bottom-up methods based on your WBS (page 193).
- Choosing your next project must always be a formal, conscious and rational decision (page 194).
- You can choose your next project without using numbers if that project is:
  - a response to floods or hurricanes (page 197) or
  - legal must-do project (page 198) or
  - an employee welfare project (page 199) or
  - a competitive advantage project (page 199).
- Relative ranking will help you to choose between projects that don't have much information (page 200).
- Choosing by number can involve you in using:
  - Payback period method (page 201)
  - ROR or ROI method (page 201)
  - NPV or DCF method (page 202)
  - Profitability Index (page 203)
  - IRR method (page 204).

INSTANT TIP

Cost estimates should be developed using the best information available. But when preparing any estimate, judgement should also be applied.

Index